Forensic Science
A Beginner's Guide

ONEWORLD BEGINNER'S GUIDES combine an original, inventive, and engaging approach with expert analysis on subjects ranging from art and history to religion and politics, and everything in-between. Innovative and affordable, books in the series are perfect for anyone curious about the way the world works and the big ideas of our time.

aesthetics
africa
american politics
anarchism
animal behaviour
anthropology
anti-capitalism
aquinas
archaeology
art
artificial intelligence
the baha'i faith
the beat generation
the bible
biodiversity
bioterror & biowarfare
the brain
british politics
the Buddha
cancer
censorship
christianity
civil liberties
classical music
climate change
cloning
the cold war
conservation
crimes against humanity
criminal psychology
critical thinking
the crusades
daoism
democracy
descartes
dewey
dyslexia
energy

engineering
the english civil wars
the enlightenment
epistemology
ethics
the european union
evolution
evolutionary psychology
existentialism
fair trade
feminism
forensic science
french literature
the french revolution
genetics
global terrorism
hinduism
history
the history of medicine
history of science
homer
humanism
huxley
international relations
iran
islamic philosophy
the islamic veil
journalism
judaism
lacan
life in the universe
literary theory
machiavelli
mafia & organized crime
magic
marx
medieval philosophy
the middle east

modern slavery
NATO
the new testament
nietzsche
nineteenth-century art
the northern ireland conflict
nutrition
oil
opera
the palestine–israeli conflict
particle physics
paul
philosophy
philosophy of mind
philosophy of religion
philosophy of science
planet earth
postmodernism
psychology
quantum physics
the qur'an
racism
rawls
reductionism
religion
renaissance art
the roman empire
the russian revolution
shakespeare
Shi'i Islam
the small arms trade
sufism
the torah
the united nations
the victorians
volcanoes
the world trade organization
world war II

Forensic Science
A Beginner's Guide

Jay Siegel

ONEWORLD

A Oneworld Book

First published by Oneworld Publications, 2009
This edition published by Oneworld Publications, 2016

ISBN 978–1–78074–824–5
eISBN 978–1–78074–825–2

Typeset by Jayvee, Trivandrum, India
Printed and bound in Great Britain by Clays Ltd, St Ives plc

Oneworld Publications
10 Bloomsbury Street
London WC1B 3SR
England

To Tommy and Ben

Contents

Illustrations   ix

Preface   xi

1 Introduction   1

2 Evidence: crime scene to crime lab   15

3 Forensic science and the law   28

4 Forensic chemistry: illicit drugs   45

5 Forensic chemistry: fires
       and explosions   66

6 Forensic chemistry: fibers
       and paint   84

7 Forensic chemistry: glass and soils   99

8 Forensic biology: pathology,
       entomology, anthropology
       and odontology   112

9 **Forensic biology: serology, DNA and blood spatter** 142

10 **Pattern evidence: fingerprints, firearms, questioned documents and hairs** 170

11 **Ethics and forensic science** 206

Conclusion 219

Further reading 222

Index 223

List of illustrations

1   Several types of search patterns used to search a
large area crime scene   18

2   Drug paraphernalia used in smoking marijuana   51

3   Blotter acid. LSD is diluted in alcohol and then
poured onto absorbent paper. The paper is then cut
into squares and eaten. A square is one dose   53

4   The fire triangle. All three elements need to be
present to start and sustain a fire   69

5   The two phases of an explosion that show how
damage can be distributed   79

6   A fiber tear match in a shirt   89

7   A reconstructed "Molotov Cocktail" bottle. The
pieces were strewn about a fire scene   103

8   Maggots feeding on necrotic tissue   126

9   Pupa stage of fly larvae   127

10   DNA double helix   154

11   A 16-loci DNA electropherogram   164

12   The fingerprint from the Madrid bombing case that
was misidentified as belonging to Brandon Mayfield   171

13   The three major classes of fingerprints   176

14   A comparison of a known fingerprint with an
inked suspect print   178

15   A photomicrograph of a bullet showing lands,
grooves, and stria   188

16   The microscopic structure of human hair   199

Preface

A lot has happened in forensic science since the first edition of this book was published in 2009. The Forensic Science Service, a company owned by the United Kingdom Government, was closed in March of 2012. With that closure, forensic science services have now been privatized or are accomplished within law enforcement agencies. In the United States, the National Academy of Sciences (NAS) issued a far-reaching, controversial report entitled "Strengthening Forensic Science in the United States: A Path Forward", which was the result of over two years of study by a seventeen-member committee made up of forensic scientists, scientific experts, and stakeholders. Many of the recommendations of the NAS Committee still reverberate today worldwide and it has spawned a Federal Government-sponsored National Commission on Forensic Science in the US.

Forensic science remains a popular subject of television shows, feature films, and books. Sherlock Holmes, who never seems to go out of style, has had somewhat of a rebirth in TV shows from the UK in a BBC production starring Benedict Cumberbatch and Martin Freeman. A less conventional take, *Elementary*, with a female Dr. Watson, is popular in the US. The American series of *CSI* shows has lost some of its glitter and popularity but at least one version is still on the air.

Although the popular media try to simplify the various areas of forensic science so the public can comprehend them, the fact is that forensic science consists of a collection of scientific applications to the fields of law enforcement and justice. Many of the major areas of forensic science are quite technical and generally difficult to comprehend fully for people who are not scientifically trained. The public's interest in forensic science remains strong and there are increasing numbers of forensic science degree programs at the bachelor's, master's and even PhD levels, especially in the UK but also in the US and other countries. Forensic science classes in secondary schools are also greatly increasing and a number of new textbooks have been published.

Despite all of the new resources available to help understand forensic science, there is still a dearth of materials aimed at the general public who don't wish to commit to taking classes or working on a degree. **Forensic Science: A Beginner's Guide** is written to fill this void. The reason for writing this book continues to be to tell the public what forensic science really is and what it isn't. The second edition has a number of new features that will hopefully make it more readable, understandable, and enjoyable. There is one new chapter on ethics that explores some of the difficulties forensic scientists face as they interface science with the justice system. The other chapters contain the most commonly encountered applications of science to legal matters. The chapters have all been updated to the latest advances and each one now begins with a real case that illustrates the principles of forensic science within that chapter.

I hope that you will enjoy reading this book and deem it worthy of your time and effort. Writing it has been a labor of love for me.

Jay A. Siegel

1
Introduction

What is forensic science?

On July 17, 1981, there was a large dance party on the ground floor of the atrium of the Hyatt Regency Hotel in Kansas City. Many of the partygoers were dancing on walkways suspended above the lobby. Suddenly, the walkway on the fourth floor collapsed onto the one on the second floor, which, in turn, collapsed onto the atrium below, killing 114 people and injuring more than 200. Engineers were called in to inspect the rubble and determine why the structures had collapsed.

In Pretoria, South Africa, police investigators found a piece of cheese in a house that had been broken into. The cheese appeared to have human bite marks in one side. A dentist matched the teeth marks to the suspect in the crime.

A man in Maryland was released from prison after serving more than eighteen years for rape. Biological evidence from the crime had been preserved and was reanalyzed using DNA typing, a technique that hadn't been developed for forensic use when the man was convicted. The forensic biologist who performed the DNA analysis declared that the biological evidence that helped convict the man could not have come from him.

In London, in 2002, the badly damaged body of a murder victim was identified when an artist's reconstructed impression of his face was recognized by members of his family.

These incidents have a common thread: they all involve the use of scientific techniques and methods of analysis. But how are these being used? Scientists use scientific methods to develop clues that answer questions about criminal or civil offenses. These matters involve the public and therefore these scientists are practicing forensic science, because the root of the term "forensic" comes from the Latin *forum*, meaning "a place for public discussion." Thus, a good definition of forensic science is "the methods and techniques of science applied to matters involving the public." When any science is applied to a matter involving the public, it is, in that instance, a forensic science. Today, forensic science has come to mean the application of the methods and techniques of science to matters involving justice and the courts. Forensic science is a big tent: almost any science can have forensic applications.

Forensic scientists and crime laboratories

Very few movies, books, or television shows depict the activities of real forensic scientists, although television broadcasts of real events, such as the O.J. Simpson trial, give viewers a glimpse of the criminal investigation process and the activities of forensic scientists. Crime scene investigation will be discussed in detail in Chapter 2. Here, we will look at what forensic scientists do and how they do it. We will also look briefly at the culture of the crime laboratory and how that affects forensic scientists' activities.

Forensic scientists have three major duties. Two – analysis of evidence and court testimony – are carried out by virtually all forensic scientists. The third, crime scene investigation, is performed by some forensic scientists, but is not a common part of the job. Analysis of scientific evidence is the bread and butter of forensic science. In most cases, forensic science laboratories analyze evidence brought to them by crime scene investigators or police investigators. This raises the interesting issue of, when they perform their analysis, how much scientists should know about the circumstances surrounding the evidence. There are two schools of thought: the first, and prevailing school, says that the examiner should have as much information as possible about the crime or incident from which the evidence came. One should never analyze evidence in a vacuum. The other school is the purely scientific one that the evidence should be analyzed completely objectively and nothing should be divulged about the evidence that would bias the examiner in any way. A couple of examples will show how this works.

Forensic chemists are often tasked with the analysis of suspected illicit drugs. A narcotics agent brings in a bag of white powder and explains to the chemist that they bought this stuff from a known cocaine dealer and want to find out how pure it is before busting the dealer. (The purity of the cocaine can reveal how far up the distribution chain the dealer is.) Before the scientist has even opened the bag, their thought process has been contaminated by the investigator's "knowledge" about the identity of the drug. The scientist must consciously avoid "finding what they are looking for" but an unknown white powder could be any one of hundreds of chemical substances. Having some idea of what the substance might be could give the scientist a path to travel and save many hours of work. Most forensic chemists opt for knowing as much as possible about the white powder before analyzing it because their testing protocols, if carried out properly, will provide ample, objective proof of the identity of the powder and they would claim that bias would not enter into the analysis in any meaningful way.

Forensic anthropologists are often called upon to identify the species that a bone or piece of bone comes from. Often this is routine, but there are many cases where it is not obvious and a good deal of careful observation is necessary. Many forensic anthropologists do not want to know anything about the circumstances under which the bone was collected; for fear that such knowledge would bias them even before they set about their analysis. In these types of examinations, analysts must rely on their own experience. There are no instruments or machines that can provide confirmation of a conclusion. The quality of the entire test depends upon the observations made by the scientist. Such decisions form part of the culture of the crime laboratory. This culture can have wide-ranging and crucial effects upon how evidence is analyzed in a particular case. We will return to this subject after looking at the other duties of a forensic scientist.

One of the interesting things about being a forensic scientist is that they have to be not only good scientists but also able to communicate their findings to the **trier of fact** – the judge or jury. The average juror in the US is scientifically literate to about eighth-grade level (13–14 years old). This presents interesting challenges to the forensic scientist, who must be able to explain difficult and complex scientific concepts and issues to people who have little or no background in science. In a courtroom, forensic scientists have the status of **expert witnesses**. An expert witness is someone with specialized knowledge, which allows them to use data or observations to draw conclusions that the average person cannot. A person need not have a PhD to be an expert witness: experience can be just as important as education.

Because of television, books, and movies, crime scene investigation (CSI) has become one of the most familiar, but misunderstood, components of the criminal justice system. Crime scene investigations are not the same as criminal investigations. Crime scene investigation involves systematically documenting and searching a crime scene for items of evidence. Once evidence is located it is preserved, documented and collected in ways that minimize contamination or spoilage. It is packed in secure containers, uniquely labeled, and either stored by the police or sent to the forensic science lab for scientific analysis. A criminal investigation is the entire process of investigating a crime. It is usually carried out under the supervision of a detective or other specialized criminal investigator. It includes the CSI process, as well as interviewing witnesses, identifying and apprehending perpetrators, gathering evidence, making a case against the suspects, making arrests, and so on.

Crime scene investigators are almost always police officers. Assignment as a crime scene investigator may take several years and lots of training. Crime scene investigation can be downright uncomfortable and even dangerous. A homicide scene can take more than twenty-four hours to investigate properly and this must be done day or night, cold or hot, wet or dry, with little sleep or food. Fire scenes can be treacherous, with no light or heat, everything soaking wet, and floors, walls, and ceilings weakened by flame and water. Animals may interfere with an outdoor crime scene investigation, especially at night, and investigation of car crashes on busy roads can be hazardous to the investigators.

Although crime scene investigation is normally carried out by specially trained technicians, it is becoming increasingly common for forensic scientists to participate. Many forensic science laboratories now work cooperatively with police departments: selected scientists will be sent to homicides or other serious crime scenes to help the technicians find, collect, and preserve the physical evidence. This is being done because forensic scientists are experts in the recognition and preservation of evidence. In addition, when the scientist has firsthand knowledge of the context in which the evidence is found, it may help in analysis and interpretation. However, having forensic scientists help with crime scene investigation also increases the opportunities for **confirmational bias** (the tendency to interpret evidence in a way that supports one's preconceptions) to creep in.

While on the subject of crime scene investigation, it is important to note the recent phenomenon of the "*CSI* Effect," named for the three US television programs that have been airing since 2001. The television-watching public has become fascinated by these and other shows, movies, and books about crime scene investigation and forensic science. However, each week, *CSI* has to tell the story of a crime and its solution within about an hour, including commercials. This involves necessary shortcuts, such as time compression, exaggerated claims about the abilities of instruments to develop data from evidence, improbable conclusions, and having CSI personnel do everything from collection of evidence to analysis, interviewing witnesses, and even making arrests. From these shows, the public has learned about how crime scenes are processed, what types of evidence are encountered, how evidence is analyzed, and what can be concluded from the forensic examination of evidence. But the shows have also given people distorted expectations and misinformation about evidence and its collection and analysis. This distortion, in turn, has rippled through the criminal justice system.

The effects are sometimes profound and far-reaching. People may have the false idea that all crimes are solvable in just a few hours. If they become victims of a crime, they question why investigators are taking so long to investigate it. The truth is that many crimes are never solved and others take many weeks or months of painstaking investigations. Jurors in criminal cases increasingly expect to see fingerprints, DNA, and other incriminating evidence in every crime. If such evidence is not there, prosecutors must explain why. And even if they do explain, jurors may punish them by finding the defendant not guilty, despite there being sufficient circumstantial evidence to support a guilty verdict. Prosecutors have responded by ordering criminal investigators to collect anything that can remotely be construed as evidence and send it to the laboratory for analysis. Crime laboratories, already overburdened and with heavy backlogs, have more items of evidence to analyze, some of which may be of dubious value or provide no help to the investigation. Criminal defense attorneys are also affected by the "*CSI* Effect": if the Government is able to produce DNA and fingerprint matches, juries may focus on that evidence, ignoring other, exculpatory evidence and thus, wrongly, find the accused guilty.

The public's knowledge of and interest in the criminal justice system and science has been raised, however imperfectly. It remains to be seen if this heightened awareness lasts beyond the life of the television shows.

Forensic laboratory systems

Many countries throughout the world have national forensic science organizations that provide such services as oversight, accreditation, continuing education, and national meetings, to name a few. Two examples, the Chartered Society of Forensic Sciences in the United Kingdom (FSS) and the American Academy of Forensic Sciences (AAFS) will suffice to illustrate the services provided by national organizations.

The Chartered Society of Forensic Scientists (UK) is a truly international, professional body, attracting more than 2,000 members from more than 60 countries. It was founded in 1959 and became a professional body in 2004. The FSS has a major role in the accreditation of university courses. They also issue Society Diplomas, whereby practitioners in specified areas of forensic investigation can achieve a professional qualification. The Society holds periodic regional and national meetings that stress professional development, research, and knowledge dissemination. The FSS publishes an international, peer-reviewed journal, *Science and Justice*, which disseminates cutting-edge developments in forensic science.

In the US, the national umbrella organization of forensic science is The **American Academy of Forensic Sciences (AAFS)**. It is organized in sections that reflect the most commonly used forensic sciences. They are:

- **Criminalistics**
- **Pathology/Biology**
- **Toxicology**
- **Odontology**
- **Physical Anthropology**
- **Engineering Sciences**
- **Jurisprudence**
- **Questioned Documents**
- **Psychiatry/Behavioral Sciences**
- **Multimedia and Digital Evidence**
- **General**

There is also an **International Association of Forensic Sciences**. This is truly an international organization, which is not affiliated with any specific country. It has a directorate made up of forensic scientists from all over the world. It holds international meetings every three years and strives to move them to disparate locations each triennial. For example, the 2011 meeting was held in Madeira, Portugal, and the 2014 meeting was in Seoul, Korea.

Crime laboratory culture

Forensic science laboratories in the UK

Until 2012, the UK Government owned a company, The **Forensic Science Service (FSS)**, that administered a network of seven forensic science laboratories. The FSS provided forensic science services to police agencies and other government agencies throughout England and Wales. It had started as an executive agency that performed forensic science services for police agencies at little or no charge. In 2005, after becoming a company, the FSS started to charge fees for its services. This opened the door for private forensic science laboratories to compete for services and the FSS started losing market share. The Government responded by putting £50 million into the company to keep it operating. Later that year it closed three of the seven laboratories and then finally announced in 2010 that it was closing the service in 2012. At that time, the FSS was £22 million in debt. Since that time, the forensic science laboratory system in the UK has been privatized, although a number of police agencies have developed in-house forensic science capabilities. The Government has retained much of the FSS archives including case files, and some samples such as microscope slides, fiber samples, and DNA samples.

Forensic science laboratories in the US

There are approximately 400 crime laboratories in the US. Most are public; they are run by departments of the Federal, State or local governments. The Federal laboratories span a number of departments and include the following:

- The Department of Justice
  - The Federal Bureau of Investigation (FBI) – The FBI has one laboratory in Quantico, Virginia. It supports investigative activities of the Bureau as well as state and local law enforcement agencies. The FBI website can be found at: www.fbi.gov/.
  - The Drug Enforcement Administration (DEA) – The DEA has a network of crime laboratories sprinkled throughout the US, and a research laboratory in Virginia. Their

responsibilities include the examination of illicit drugs seized by DEA agents and task forces made up of DEA agents and local law enforcement agents. They also support interdiction of drugs in other countries that have major drug export activity to the US. www.usdoj.gov/dea/.

- Department of Homeland Security
  - Bureau of Alcohol, Tobacco, Firearms and Explosives (BATF) – The ATF has three laboratories and a unique fire-research laboratory The ATF has wide-ranging activities supported by its laboratories. These include enforcement of alcohol tax regulations, firearms production, import and export, and tobacco commerce and taxes. They also have expertise in fires and explosions analysis and investigation. www.atf.treas.gov.
  - Secret Service (USSS) – And you thought that all they did was guard the President! In addition to its protective functions, the USSS is responsible for protecting the US currency and, by extension, credit cards and other monetary instruments. They investigate frauds and counterfeiting operations, supported by their laboratory in Washington, DC. www.ustreas.gov/usss/index.shtml.

- Department of the Treasury
  - Internal Revenue Service (IRS) – The IRS has a laboratory in Chicago that specializes in questioned document work including handwriting, inks, papers, and other writing instruments. Their major responsibility is tax collection enforcement. www.irs.gov/

- Department of the Interior
  - US Fish and Wildlife Service (USFWS) – Why would the FWS need a crime laboratory? In fact, their laboratory in Ashland, Oregon, has some of the world's leading experts in animal forensics. This laboratory supports the

activities of FWS agents who are responsible for enforcing laws against illegal hunting and poaching on Federal lands. Check out the laboratory on the web at: www.laboratory. fws.gov/.

- US Postal Service (USPS) – The US Postal Service is a quasi-governmental agency. It is partially funded by the US Government but is a sort of private enterprise. It has a laboratory in Washington, DC, that supports the mail functions of the USPS. www.usps.com/postalinspectors/crimelab.htm.

Every state in the US has some form of crime laboratory system. These range from a single laboratory for Wyoming to more than fifty public laboratories in California. The organizational structures of crime laboratories also differ from state to state. There are three basic governmental structures that administer public laboratories: State, county, and city laboratories. Most commonly, statewide laboratories are administered by the State Police. In Michigan, for example, the State Police run a network of seven regional crime laboratories, each of which covers a geographic region of the state. Some states, such as California, have a Department of Justice that maintains a network of forensic science laboratories.

Forensic science laboratories in Australia

In Australia, a country about the size of the US but with less than one tenth of the population, there is at least one forensic science laboratory in each state. For example, in New South Wales, the largest state in Australia, the State Police have a laboratory that does some analyses such as firearms and fingerprints. There is also a separate state laboratory that analyzes illicit drugs and still another one for other evidence. In South Australia, there is an excellent, full-service crime laboratory in Adelaide. The other states also have laboratories. In addition, there is one Federal laboratory that supports the Federal Police. This full-service laboratory is in Canberra, the capital of Australia.

The work environment

Forensic scientists do not operate in a vacuum. The culture and environment of the crime laboratory can have a profound effect on how the work gets done. The pressures on scientists from police investigators, prosecutors, and defense attorneys, as well as from the adversarial system under which they must function, can cause covert – or even overt – bias to creep in and the science to become compromised. Occasionally, there are extreme cases where bias becomes so pervasive that the scientist becomes corrupted by it. Such is the case of Fred Zain.

Zain spent many years working as a forensic scientist in the West Virginia Department of Public Safety Crime Laboratory. He was well respected, and became something of a forensic science "star." Prosecutors and detectives preferred him, because he always seemed to find the evidence that convicted the people they focused on. Over the years, he rose through the ranks to the position of chief of the serology (blood analysis) section of the lab. The problem was that he apparently misrepresented and mishandled some of the evidence he received. He regularly reported results that were either from evidence he didn't test (a practice called **dry-labbing**) or were just plain wrong. By all accounts, he continued this practice for years, until he was finally caught out in a lie.

Fred Zain's transgressions were particularly serious but his was by no means an isolated case. Such lapses could happen anywhere where there is lax supervision of laboratory personnel. There have been and continue to be abuses of the forensic science system by forensic scientists worldwide. The Morin case in Canada had many examples of lost and misplaced evidence, improper procedures, and improper testimony. The Splatt case in Australia was a notorious example of how prosecutors may proceed against someone with faulty scientific evidence and how a system of checks and balances may not work. The Sir Roy Meadow affair, in England, stands as an example of alleged malpractice by a physician in several forensic cases. Even though such cases are few, they are often very public and magnify the problems that occur in forensic science. The vast majority of forensic scientists claim to be able to function effectively, maintaining a degree of objectivity and helping the evidence tell its story without regard to which side gets the benefit. It is only a few that allow bias to creep in and allow themselves to become advocates instead of disinterested scientists.

In spite of all of these issues and problems, the vast majority of forensic scientists love their work. Interviews with forensic scientists have shown high levels of job satisfaction, because they have a chance to use their interest and background in science to help tackle serious crime, because they love to solve problems, and because of the public nature of their jobs in a courtroom.

Overall, forensic science systems tend to be decentralized, under the control of law enforcement agencies, and lacking consistent standards of operating procedures and analytical methods. Many laboratories are understaffed and overworked and, at least in the US, this has resulted in very large backlogs of cases that cause results to be delayed for months. Few forensic science systems have mandatory accreditation of their laboratories or certification of individual analysts. This has led to uneven levels of competence among scientists and sometimes a lack of accountability when mistakes are made. There is also no uniform code of ethics that applies to the entire profession of forensic science. In the laboratory, forensic scientists tend to react to crime: evidence is normally brought to the laboratory by scene of crime officers. It is relatively rare for scientists to venture out to crime scenes and collect evidence. This will be explored in more detail in the next chapter, which deals with the collection and processing of evidence.

2

Evidence: crime scene to crime lab

In Chapter 1, crime investigation was briefly described. In this chapter, the broader topic of evidence is discussed. Much of the evidence in a crime can be found at the scene of the incident and, at least initially, a criminal investigation will be concentrated on the scene. It must be remembered, however, that, in many cases, evidence of a crime may be found at other locations, such as the home or business of the victim(s) or suspect(s). For example, a shoeprint outside a house that has been broken into may be discovered outside a window. When a suspect is apprehended, a search of his home may reveal a pair of shoes whose soles have shoeprint pattern similar to the one at the scene and may also contain mud that may be linked to the scene. This shoe can then be compared to the shoeprint and the mud can be compared to soil in which the shoeprint is located. Regardless of the location of the evidence, it can be sent to a forensic science laboratory where it will be analyzed. Remember that, in the vast majority of cases, the scientists who analyze the evidence are not the same as the crime scene investigators who collect it.

The criminal investigation process

For a criminal investigation to take place, the crime must come to the attention of the police. A victim of a crime may call the police, a witness to a crime may tell the police, or a police officer may witness a crime. In some cases, the police may set up circumstances in which a crime is committed (a "sting" operation). Once the police become aware of a crime, a sequence of steps starts, some of which happen simultaneously (what follows is, of course, US procedure; arrangements vary in different countries):

- A police officer will go to the crime scene, attend to the injured and cordon off the scene.
- Witnesses/victims who are present will be interviewed.
- If there is a good likelihood that the perpetrator of the crime is still in the vicinity, a **hot search** will take place.
- If there is a dead body, a forensic pathologist from the medical examiner's or coroner's office will be dispatched to the scene to examine the body and gather data to help estimate the time since death (the post-mortem interval).
- The crime scene unit will be dispatched. Depending upon the size of the police department (remembering that crime scene technicians are usually police officers), the unit may consist of a photographer and one or more technicians who will search for evidence, document it, collect it, put it in secure packaging, and take it to the property room of the police department. The systematic search of a crime scene cannot stop and can take hours or days. A television show that depicted a real, major crime scene investigation from start to finish wouldn't do very well in the ratings!
- Police investigators (usually detectives if the police department is large enough) will attend the crime scene to look at the evidence and start investigating the crime. They will also interview witnesses and search beyond the scene for other evidence and witnesses and suspects (a **cold search**). A police investigator will retrieve the evidence from the property room and take it to the forensic science laboratory where it will be logged and analyzed by forensic scientists.

- When a suspect has been identified, police investigators will meet the prosecutor to go over the case and determine if there is sufficient evidence to go forward. If there is, a grand jury may be convened or a preliminary hearing conducted to determine if there is sufficient evidence to try the accused.

This is, of course, little more than an outline of how a criminal investigation is carried out.

The search for physical evidence and clues at a crime scene is similar to the reconstruction of a historical event, or like an archaeological investigation, in which the ruins of a past civilization are carefully unearthed to gain clues about its culture. The difference in a crime scene investigation is that the events are much more recent. The CSI team and the criminal investigators must carefully sift through the scene to identify the pieces of evidence that help tell the story of how the crime was committed and by whom.

Some of the principles that guide archaeologists as they search ancient sites are also used in searching a crime scene. First, it is very easy to contaminate a crime scene. Every time a person walks into a room, they bring in material from outside: bits of soil, fibers, dandruff, and so on. This extraneous material could be confused with evidence. When that person leaves the room, they may carry out material that might be evidence. In searching a crime scene, contamination must be minimized, although it cannot be completely eliminated because people have to search the scene, record it, and collect evidence, and any contact causes some contamination.

Second, the crime scene must be searched systematically. Imagine you lose a valuable ring in your backyard. How do you make sure that you have checked every square inch? You probably would set up a pattern and follow it; crime scene investigators do the same thing. Some of the more common search patterns are shown in Figure 1. The exact pattern used will be deter-

Figure 1 Several types of search patterns used to search a large area crime scene

mined partly by the size and location of the scene and partly by the personnel available. On April 17, 1984, there was a demonstration outside the Libyan Embassy in London. Suddenly, shots rang out from inside the embassy, fatally wounding Yvonne Fletcher, a police officer on duty outside. When Fletcher's body underwent a post-mortem, it was discovered that the bullet that had killed her was missing. It was not in or on the body, nor on the trolley that had carried the body, nor in the ambulance. More than fifty police officers, spaced no more than two feet apart, gathered at one end of the courtyard outside the embassy and crawled on their hands and knees to search for the bullet, which was found.

Third, just as in an excavation of a historical site, a crime scene must be fully documented. Each piece of evidence must be noted, along with the exact location where it was found. Measurements fix the evidence with respect to a permanent object such as a wall or window and the evidence is plotted on a sketch of the scene, which is later converted to a scale drawing. Photography is an essential part of crime scene documentation. Increasingly, investigators use digital photography in conjunction with videotaping of the scene. These complement, but do not completely replace, the scale drawings.

Finally, evidence must be collected without damaging or destroying it. For example, if liquid blood is placed in an airtight container, it will putrefy and the components that are used for identification may be destroyed. Living marijuana plants must be placed in a permeable container so they do not spoil. Contamination by investigating personnel must be minimized to avoid spoiling or ruining evidence. Table 1 shows the differences between an excavation and a crime scene investigation.

Table 1 Excavation v. investigation

Excavation	Investigation
• Contains clues (artifacts)	• Contains clues (evidence)
• Tries to answer:	• Tries to answer:
• Who lived there?	• What happened? A crime?
• When was it inhabited?	• Who was there?
• When and why was it abandoned?	• Was there a victim there? Who?
• How did the inhabitants live?	• Who was the perpetrator(s)?

Evidence

It could be fairly said that the unit of currency in a criminal investigation is **evidence**. Law books define evidence as *anything that can make a fact/proposition more or less likely than it would have been absent the evidence.* Think of evidence as being *anything that helps prove or disprove something about the crime being investigated.* Evidence can be objects like guns or drugs or blood. It can also be circumstances such as a location or an alibi. It can also be testimony and opinions. In this chapter, we will discuss different types of evidence. In Chapter 3, we will discuss how evidence is admitted into court.

Types of evidence

There are a number of ways that evidence can be classified and a given piece of evidence can fall into more than one category:

- **Real, demonstrative, testimonial**
- **Known v. unknown**
- **Class v. individual**

Real, demonstrative, testimonial evidence

Real evidence arises directly from criminal activity: examples are blood, fingerprints, fibers, and drugs. **Demonstrative evidence** is generated by police investigators or witnesses to illustrate or graphically depict evidence: examples are crime scene sketches, photographs, models, and videotapes of a crime scene. There is a crucial difference: demonstrative evidence is created after the crime has occurred, not generated by the criminal activity itself. Consequently, the rules on admissibility of demonstrative evidence are different than for real evidence. **Testimonial evidence** is oral or written: an eyewitness to a bank robbery can testify that at 4 p.m. she saw someone wearing blue jeans and a white T-shirt run out of the bank, holding a large sack and shooting a gun back into the bank. The gun, the sack, and her statement about what she witnessed will be evidence at the trial. Another example of testimonial evidence arises from a polygraph (or similar) test. The polygraph measures changes in certain nervous system functions as a person answers questions. These changes are shown on a chart. The evidence, however, is the oral or written testimony of the polygraph examiner, who gives their interpretation of what the marks on the chart mean and their conclusions about the truth or deception of the answers given by the subject.

Known v. unknown evidence

In the evaluation of physical evidence, the most important question is: *what or who is the source of this evidence?* If evidence is found at a crime scene or elsewhere, this question is always asked. If the answer is *I don't know*, the evidence is classified as unknown. The answer to this vital question may depend upon when it is asked. For the purposes of recovery and analysis of the evidence, the question is asked when the evidence is found. For example, a fingerprint is found on a window at the scene of a burglary. The detective asks: "Who does this fingerprint belong to?" The answer, at that time, is "We don't know." Thus, the fingerprint is unknown evidence.

Why is it important to establish whether evidence is known or unknown? Because it guides investigators and forensic scientists in determining what additional evidence is needed as the case develops. Finding a fingerprint at a crime scene is not very helpful (forensic scientists and lawyers would say it is "not very probative") if there is no known fingerprint with which to compare it. When a suspect is identified, the fingerprint examiner can obtain known fingerprints and compare them to the unknown print to see if it can be determined whether the suspect left that print at the scene. (Note: even if the print matches the suspect's, it doesn't prove that they committed the burglary and it doesn't show when the print was left on the window. It only proves that the suspect left that print at some time in the past.)

Let's look at a more complicated case. A pedestrian, walking across a busy street, is hit by a car and dies instantly. The driver stops briefly but, believing there are no witnesses, quickly drives away. However, there is a witness, who phones the police with a description of the car but not its license plate. Shortly afterwards, a car matching the description is stopped for speeding and the driver arrested on suspicion of being involved in the hit-and-run accident. The body of the victim is taken to the medical examiner's laboratory, where an autopsy is performed. His clothes are taken to the forensic science laboratory, where his blue cotton coat is carefully inspected; it has smears of white paint and contains some glass fragments. The suspect car is impounded and taken to a police garage, where it is inspected. The left front fender is damaged and some paint is missing. Some blue fibers are embedded in the damaged area. The left front headlight is broken and part of the lens is missing. Table 2 shows how investigators and forensic scientists determine the classification of each piece of evidence.

Table 2 Unknown evidence v. known evidence

Unknown evidence	Known evidence
White paint smears found on coat	White paint from damaged area of car
Glass fragments found in the coat	Glass taken from the broken headlight
Blue fibers taken from damaged area of car	Fibers taken from victim's coat

For every piece of unknown evidence in this case (that is, evidence whose source is initially unknown), there exists known evidence with which it can be compared. The results of these comparisons will give forensic scientists data from which conclusions can be drawn about the source of the pieces of unknown evidence. For example, a paint chemist would perform physical and chemical tests on the paint smears on the coat and on known paint taken from the car. If the results of the tests are the same for both the unknown and known paints, the forensic scientist can conclude that the paint smears on the coat *could have* originated from the automobile suspected of being involved in the incident. This is not the same as concluding that this particular car was the *only* one that could have been the source of the paint smears: there are probably thousands of similar vehicles with the same type of paint. Similar reasoning can be used for the analysis of the glass fragments found in the victim's coat, the glass from the broken headlight, and for fibers embedded in the damaged area of the car compared to fibers taken from the victim's coat.

Class v. individual evidence

This concept, of **individualizing** forensic evidence, is very important. The term implies that it is possible to state – to a reasonable degree of scientific certainty – that an object came from one particular source and not from any other. For certain types of forensic evidence, including fingerprints, firearms and toolmarks, and handwriting, this concept has been adopted and embraced for many years. For more than a hundred years, qualified fingerprint examiners have been testifying that a fingerprint obtained from an object at a crime scene came from a particular finger of a particular person. In such cases, the conclusions are based upon the examiner's careful observation and many years of experience, not upon the results of exhaustive empirical research that would establish that every fingerprint is demonstrably distinguishable from every other fingerprint. It is not possible to prove that all fingerprints differ from all others.

Even the science of DNA typing has embraced the concept of individualization, but in a different way. Modern DNA typing is accomplished by determining the particular variant of DNA present at a number of locations on the genome. (Statistical data on the frequency of each variant at each location exists.) Since the type of DNA at each of these locations has been shown to be independent of the others, the probability of having a particular variant at each location can be multiplied by the other probabilities. This yields an incredibly small overall probability of having a particular combined DNA type. These statistics are interpreted as being the chance that two, randomly chosen, people would have the same DNA type. The argument is that, since these chances are so small, finding the same DNA type in evidence as in a suspect amounts to *de facto* individualization. However, this is not a proper interpretation of these statistics and does not justify a conclusion of absolute individualization.

References to individualization in later chapters will assume that it is possible, because that is the prevailing opinion among forensic scientists and because such conclusions are routinely accepted in courts. You should, however, keep these points in mind when considering individualization. From the standpoint of the importance of evidence in a criminal investigation and/ or trial, the issue of class versus individual evidence is most important.

The analysis of evidence involves two processes: **identification** and **comparison**. Identification is always made in the process of analysis. In those cases where an object from a known source is to be linked to evidentiary samples, such as a bullet test-fired from a weapon and a bullet taken from the victim of a homicide, a comparison test will be performed. Or consider a bag of white powder submitted to a crime laboratory by a criminal investigator, who found it among a stash of balances, baggies, tape, scoops, and various containers at the home of a suspected drug dealer. The investigator may ask the forensic scientist a number of questions: What is it? Is it a pure substance? How much is there? Could it have come from a large vat of white powder found at the same location?

The first three questions concern the identification of the material in the bag. The forensic scientist and crime investigators need to know if this bag contains an illicit drug and, if so, its identity, quantity, and purity need to be determined. This information is needed for prosecution and perhaps intelligence purposes. The physical and chemical tests performed on the white powder help to classify it. For example, the tests could show that the bag contains 50g of powder that is 50% heroin and 50% sugar. This tells us what the powder is, how pure it is and how much there is. These are all **class properties**. The last question asks about the source of this powder. For intelligence purposes, it may be important for the police to know that the powder in question was part of a larger quantity of 50% heroin.

They may know who owns the large vat of powder and want to link the 50g bag with that: they hope to individualize the small bag of powder to the larger source. Unfortunately, in this case this is not possible. There is nothing unique about a 50g bag of 50% heroin: there could be hundreds of such bags.

Let's go back to the bullet that was recovered from the victim of the shooting. As a bullet is fired, it picks up microscopic markings on its surface, due to imperfections on the inside of the barrel. Firearms examiners claim that each barrel has unique imperfections and thus all bullets fired from a particular weapon will have a characteristic set of microscopic markings. If the suspected weapon is test-fired with ammunition of the same type as the bullet recovered from the crime scene, a microscope can be used to compare the markings on the bullets side by side. If there are enough similar characteristics (and no unexplained differences) to satisfy the firearms examiner, it can be reasonably concluded that the two bullets were fired from the same weapon. The bullet from the victim has been individualized; it has been put into a class of one, because the bullet has **unique** or **individual** characteristics.

Not all types of physical evidence have characteristics that enable individualization. Table 3 lists some common types of

Table 3 Potentially individualizable evidence v. class evidence

Potentially individualizable evidence	Class evidence
Bullets and certain tools	Hairs*
Fingerprints (also palm prints and footprints)	Single fibers
Handwriting	Soil
Large paint chips or pieces of glass (by fracture matching)	Tiny paint chips or glass pieces
Blood and body fluids (DNA typing only)	Inks and dyes

* If the hair contains a root, cellular DNA may be extracted. This can lead to individualization of the hair to a particular individual.

evidence that have the **potential** for individualization. Some of these will be discussed in later chapters. Where individualization is possible, a comparison test must be performed to compare the unique characteristics of the known and unknown evidence. If no known evidence is available for comparison, the unknown evidence cannot be individualized.

A crime scene can be thought of as a recent historical site that must be processed in ways that are similar to archaeological investigations. The search must be systematic and thoroughly documented. Unnecessary intrusions can lead to contamination and must be minimized. The location of objects and people at a crime scene relative to others is very important. One major difference between a crime scene and an archaeological site is the legal requirement of **chain of custody**. This is both a document and a process that protects evidence, makes apparent any attempts to tamper with evidence, and records who possessed the evidence at any given time. Evidence can be classified in a number of ways. The most important classification system divides evidence into **class** or **individual**. The classification that a piece of evidence falls into governs the proper conclusions that can be made about its relationship with a suspected source. Class evidence cannot be associated with one particular object or person. Individual evidence can be compared with an object from a known source and, if there are sufficient unique characteristics in common, it can be concluded that the evidence arose from that source. This conclusion is based upon the premise that the unique characteristics reduce the probability of its coming from another source to a level that can be considered insignificant. The individualization of biological evidence by employing DNA typing takes advantage of the development of databases that give rise to known population frequencies for all the DNA types that are examined forensically. This permits the examiner to relate the frequency of occurrence of a particular DNA type in the human population. If this frequency is rare enough, a conclusion of individuality may be justified.

The principle that makes forensic science so unique is that the collection and analysis of evidence is only part of the story. Where the rubber really meets the road is in the courtroom. The best science in the world cannot make up for ineffective expert witnesses. There is also the issue of what evidence is admissible in court and how it is admitted. Forensic science and the law will be considered in the next chapter.

3
Forensic science and the law

Scientific evidence is analyzed in the laboratory, or sometimes at the crime scene, but the real drama is played out in the courtroom. This is what makes forensic science forensic. All legal systems put constraints on what evidence will be received at trial and who will present evidence. A witness is called to a trial by a subpoena – an order to appear in court concerning a specific matter on a specific date – signed by a judge. Ignoring a subpoena can put one in contempt of court and could result in a jail sentence. Expert witnesses must produce all the documents that are relevant to the case: reports, charts, graphs, and notes made during their analysis of the evidence. This chapter will discuss the unique nature of scientific and technical evidence and how it is treated.

Criminal court systems

Many countries have layered court systems. In the UK, there are two layers of criminal trial court. The lower court is the Magistrate's Court, where less serious offenses are usually tried. In the US, these are often called District Courts. The higher-level criminal court in the UK is the Crown Court. This court hears appeals from the Magistrate's Court and is the court of first hearing for more serious crimes. In the US, these are often called Superior or Circuit Courts.

The UK has three levels of appeals court: the Queen's Bench court can hear appeals from summary trials held in the Magistrate's Court; the Court of Appeal hears appeals from the Crown Courts; and the House of Lords hears appeals from both other appeals courts. In the US, there are one or two layers of appeals courts in each state, and the Supreme Court, which can hear appeals from the highest state or Federal courts.

Trial procedure is much the same in the UK, US, and courts worldwide. A jury is selected, then there are opening statements by the prosecutor, evidence introduced by the prosecutor through witnesses, who may be cross-examined by the defense, then an opening statement from the defense, which may choose to introduce evidence and put on witnesses who are subject to cross-examination by the prosecutor. Closing statements and a verdict end the trial.

The rules of evidence

In Chapter 2, we learned that evidence can be defined as anything that makes a fact or proposition more or less likely; it tends to prove or disprove something about the issue at hand. However, just because some evidence may appear to prove something about the case, that doesn't mean it will be automatically admitted into court during a hearing or trial. The UK and US jurisprudence systems have rules governing the admissibility of evidence that go back centuries and are rooted in English common law. These rules tend to limit the amount and types of evidence that can be admitted, for many reasons. To understand these reasons, it is important to understand who the actors in a trial are and what their roles are.

Arguably, the most important person in a trial is the so-called **trier of fact**. The trier of fact is the party who determines the guilt or innocence of the accused. If the trial is heard before a jury, the members of the jury are collectively the trier of fact; in a bench trial, the judge is the trier of fact. In a jury trial, the jury applies the facts of the case that they hear or see in court to the law, as instructed by the judge, and determines if the defendant is guilty. In a bench trial, that duty is the judge's. Juries do not interpret the law, or make rulings or decisions concerning matters of law. That is a matter for the judge. The prosecution and defense in a criminal trial, or the plaintiff and defense in a civil trial, are the parties in the case. Nothing that is said during the trial by the attorneys for the parties in a case is evidence. Evidence is only presented by witnesses or as objects, such as documents, that are admitted during the trial.

Many of the rules governing evidence were created to protect the trier of fact, especially a jury. For example, there are rules to ensure that the evidence being offered is reliable. Other rules prevent the jury's time being wasted, by limiting the admission of needless or cumulative evidence. Yet other rules protect the rights of the accused by limiting character evidence or evidence that is prejudicial. A description of all of the rules of evidence is beyond the scope of this book but a few of the more important ones, that apply to all evidence, will be described, with an emphasis on the special rules that apply to scientific or technical evidence.

The two big rules: relevance and competence

All evidence that is both relevant and competent is admissible in court. If evidence is not relevant, it is not admissible, even if it is competent. Although this sounds simple, the devil is in the details and courts spend a good deal of time determining if evidence meets all the tests of relevance and competence.

There are two components to relevance: materiality and probativeness. Both tests must be met for the evidence to be admitted. Evidence is material if it has something to do with the case that is being tried. The fact that a defendant in a case of burglary was previously arrested for theft is not material to the present case. This is one of the reasons that juries are not allowed to know of a defendant's previous criminal record. The requirement that evidence is authenticated and accounted for from the time it is discovered at a crime until it gets to court is also part of materiality. If the police cannot prove that the gun being admitted as evidence is the one that was used in the homicide, it is not material to the case. Probativeness means that the evidence must prove something about the case: the mere fact that the accused was in the vicinity of a crime might not prove anything about their guilt.

Competence has a different meaning in jurisprudence than in other contexts. It doesn't mean the ability to do something well: in law, competence is a collection of rules and constraints. Some constraints are concerned with the violation of certain privileges. For example, there are two common law privileges related to marriage: if a partner makes incriminating statements to their spouse, the spouse may be protected from having to testify against their partner; and even if the spouse wants to testify, their partner may be able to prevent it. Likewise, some confessions made to a priest in the confessional, or to a lawyer who is retained as counsel, may be kept out of court. There are other rules of competence, including prejudice and hearsay. We will discuss hearsay later, in conjunction with laboratory reports of analysis. It is important to emphasize that evidence must both pass competence tests *and* be relevant to be admitted into court.

Admissibility of scientific or technical evidence

Have you ever seen a commercial on television where someone is trying to sell a medicine or other consumer product? Sometimes the speaker wears a white lab coat and, if the product is medical, sports a stethoscope. The marketing ploy is, of course, that the speaker is a doctor or scientist and if a scientist is selling this product it must be good. People tend to believe what scientists say; they are supposed to be smart, experts in their field, and their statements to have a ring of truth about them. This is also true in court. Members of a jury (or the judge) tend to put great weight on the testimony of scientists. The average juror does not possess the technical knowledge to determine whether what the scientist says is true so it is accepted without question. There is potential danger in this. Sometimes scientists give misleading or untruthful testimony and the jury can reach wrong conclusions based on what they hear. Scientists and technical experts can make mistakes or they can purposely mislead the trier of fact because they would benefit financially from doing so. For these reasons, expert testimony is subject to rules of admissibility that go beyond the rules mentioned previously for other types of evidence. Not only must expert testimony be relevant and competent, it must also pass other tests that have been enacted only for scientific or technical matters. In the United Kingdom and the United States, these special rules have been developed both through court decisions and legislation. The following discourse traces the development of the set of rules that apply to scientific and technical evidence in the United States.

The Frye Rule

Prior to 1923, scientific and technical evidence was treated pretty much the same as other types; it had to pass tests of relevance and competence. In 1923, a trial took place in Federal Court in Washington, DC, that changed the admissibility of scientific and technical evidence forever in Federal cases and in many states. James Frye was on trial for murder. To help bolster his contention of innocence, he submitted himself to a sort of primitive polygraph test. The modern polygraph measures several functions such as blood pressure and respiration and how they change when a person is being deceptive when answering questions. The instrument that Frye was tested on measured only one function (Systolic Blood Pressure Test). The examiner who administered the test to Frye concluded that he was being truthful when he answered questions that indicated that he was not guilty of the murder. Frye sought to have the results of this test admitted into court as proof of his innocence. The prosecutor objected to this "scientific" evidence on the grounds that the underlying principle of this test – that the instrument could detect deception by recording changes in blood pressure response – was not accepted as valid by experts in the relevant fields of science. His argument was that, if experts could not agree about the reliability of the test, how could jurors reasonably rely on the test results? The jurors would be forced to speculate about the truth of the results of the test and therefore the guilt or innocence of Frye. They would have to make decisions about a scientific test about which they did not have the necessary knowledge, and thus might easily make a mistake in interpretation of the results of the test. In ruling upon the admissibility of the blood pressure test, the judge sided with the prosecutor and stated:

> *Just when a scientific principle or discovery crosses the line between the experimental and demonstrable stages is difficult to define. Somewhere in this twilight zone the evidentiary force of the principle must be recognized, and, while courts will go a long way in admitting expert testimony deduced from a well-recognized scientific principle or discovery,*

> *the thing from which the deduction is made must be sufficiently estab-*
> *lished to have gained general acceptance in the particular field to which*
> *it belongs.*

> *(Frye v. United States, 293F. 1013, 1014 (D.C. Cir. 1923))*

A new standard for admissibility of scientific evidence arose from this case. It is called the **general acceptance** standard. It means that, whenever a party seeks to introduce a new scientific test or technique, the relevant scientific community must first generally accept it. In the case of the Systolic Blood Pressure Deception Test mentioned in the *Frye* case, the relevant scientific community would be psychologists, anatomists, and neurophysiologists. One of the problems with the *Frye* decision was that the judge in the case never defined what he meant by "general acceptance." Over the intervening years since *Frye*, general acceptance has come to mean that the technique has been published in a peer-reviewed journal. This is a scientific journal in which decisions about whether to publish a manuscript are made by peer scientists in the same field as the manuscript. Peer-reviewed journals are considered the most reliable types of publications for scientific matters. The general acceptance test embodied in the *Frye* case was eventually adopted by more than twenty-five states in the US and by many, if not all, Federal Courts.

Federal Rules of Evidence

In the US, all courts operate according to a set of rules of evidence. In Federal Courts, these rules are promulgated by the US Congress and are generally binding only on the Federal Courts. State courts do not have to abide by these rules unless they affect fundamental rights guaranteed by the US Constitution. These rules govern virtually all situations involving evidence, including who presents it, how it is presented, and limitations on its admissibility. During the twentieth century, the **Federal Rules**

of Evidence (**FREs**) had become outmoded and outdated. In 1976, Congress extensively changed them. Some of these rules refer specifically to scientific evidence. They specify who shall present it, under what conditions it may be admitted, and what data shall be presented and relied on to reach expert conclusions. An extensive discussion of these changes is beyond the scope of this book, but one revised rule, FRE 702, warrants discussion because it is pivotal in controlling the admission of scientific and technical evidence. This rule has undergone some changes since it was first written in 1976, but its essence is the same. Today, it reads:

> *If scientific, technical, or other specialized knowledge will assist the trier of fact to understand the evidence or to determine a fact in issue, a witness qualified as an expert by knowledge, skill, experience, training, or education, may testify thereto in the form of an opinion or otherwise, if (1) the testimony is based upon sufficient facts or data, (2) the testimony is the product of reliable principles and methods, and (3) the witness has applied the principles and methods reliably to the facts of the case.*

Although the rule is brief, it has a number of important implications. It reaffirms the relevancy standard for scientific evidence (*will assist the trier of fact*) but goes further to require a showing that the data being used to support the conclusions is sufficient and that the science that underlies the testimony must be reliable (one way to do this is to assure general acceptance by the relevant scientific community). Further, there must be proof that the scientific methods and principles were correctly applied in a particular case.

Once Congress passed these new FREs, they became the law for all Federal Courts. Although the reformulated rules did not apply to state courts, nonetheless most states adopted many of these rules in whole or in part. Since the new FREs were promulgated, many Federal Courts have chosen to ignore them when making decisions about the admissibility of novel scientific evidence, instead continuing to rely on the *Frye* standard. This practice lasted until 1993 when the *Daubert v. Merrell Dow* case occurred.

Daubert v. Merrell Dow

The *Daubert* case is an example of a **toxic tort**. A tort is a type of civil infraction. It is a harm to a person or people by another person or people. A toxic tort is a harm that is alleged to have been caused by a dangerous or poisonous substance. Mrs. Daubert was a pregnant woman whose doctor prescribed **Bendectin**, a drug that was commonly prescribed to relieve nausea among women in their first trimester of pregnancy. In 1993, Mrs. Daubert ultimately gave birth to a baby who had birth defects. She subsequently had another baby, also with birth defects, also after she took Bendectin. She sued the manufacturer of Bendectin, the Merrell Dow Company, in Federal Court, claiming that the drug was the cause of the birth defects in her babies. The Merrell Dow Company denied that their drug caused the birth defects and a trial ensued. The case was heard in Federal Court rather than State Court because the Merrell Dow Company engages in interstate commerce and Federal Courts have jurisdiction in such situations.

The biochemical mechanisms that result in birth defects are not well known and there was no way at that time to prove medically that Bendectin caused birth defects. As a result, the plaintiff, Mrs. Daubert, had to use **epidemiology**, the large-scale study of disease, to prove her case. This is the same type of strategy that has been used in court to try to establish that cigarettes cause cancer. Essentially, the plaintiff retained epidemiologists to gather data about the number of women who gave birth to babies with birth defects, the number of women who took Bendectin while pregnant, and the number of women who took Bendectin while pregnant and gave birth to babies with birth defects. They then took this data and used statistics to determine if there was a **statistically significant** increase in the number of birth defects in babies from women who took Bendectin compared to the number in women who did not take Bendectin. Mrs. Daubert's statisticians determined that there was an increase and that it was statistically significant, thereby implicating Bendectin in the birth defects. Merrell Dow's statisticians determined from approximately the same data, but using different statistical methods for their analysis, that there was no statistically significant difference in birth defects with and without Bendectin.

When Mrs. Daubert's epidemiologists were going to offer their testimony, the defense objected on the grounds that her scientists did not use *generally accepted* methods of statistics in order to reach their conclusions and, because of that, their testimony should not be admitted. The defense was, in effect, invoking the Frye Rule. The judge agreed with the defense and disallowed the plaintiff's testimony. Since her statisticians could not testify about their data, the plaintiff had insufficient evidence to continue to press the case and the judge directed the jury to return a verdict in favor of Merrell Dow, thus ending the trial. Mrs. Daubert's lawyers appealed the decision on the grounds that the trial judge used the wrong standard of admissibility of the scientific evidence. They claimed that the judge should have used the FREs as the standard of admissibility and not the *Frye* standard.

The United States Supreme Court agreed to hear the appeal and ultimately agreed with Mrs. Daubert. They remanded the case back to the trial court for a re-hearing and directed the judge to use the Federal Rules of Evidence to make his determination on the admissibility of the plaintiff's statistical evidence. The Supreme Court decision stated that the *Frye* standard no longer applied to the Federal Courts and that it was too restrictive. They determined that FRE 702 put the responsibility on the judge to act as a "gatekeeper" and determine the admissibility of scientific evidence on broader grounds. They concluded that scientific evidence must be reliable and that the test for reliability was to be scientific validity. The Justices concluded that there were many possible tests of scientific validity beyond general acceptance and, in their opinion about the case, listed a few:

- **Falsifiability**: This concept refers to testing a new theory or method. When a new scientific theory is proposed, it is subjected to rigorous experimentation that attempts to prove that the theory is false or doesn't work. If repeated attempts to prove it false fail, this provides evidence that the theory is valid. An example would be the theory that gravity on earth pulls all objects towards the center of the earth. If someone drops a hammer on earth, it should fall to the ground. Repeated tests of this theory show that a dropped hammer will always fall down and not up. Since no examples of the theory being false have been shown, it must be true.
- **Known error rates**: During the development of a new technique or method, a scientist will determine or estimate the frequency of errors and their types when the method is used. All scientific tests and methods are subject to errors. Knowing the frequency of these errors will help the trier of fact determine the validity of the method. If tests show that a particular method of analysis has a very low error rate, it can be relied upon to a high degree.
- **Peer review**: The Supreme Court recognized the value of publishing and peer review of scientific methods and techniques and they included it in their suggested means of assessing scientific validity.
- **General acceptance**: The Supreme Court didn't say that the *Frye* standard wasn't a valid means of assessing scientific

validity, only that it cannot be the sole means of doing so. They recognized that scientific consensus has significant value in evaluating a new scientific technique.

Since the Supreme Court ruling in *Daubert*, most states have adopted the decision in whole or in part. There are still a few *Frye* states, but *Daubert* has essentially become the principal means for evaluating the admissibility of scientific and technical evidence. Further court decisions have clarified and extended *Daubert* since 1993 and there are still test cases being prepared to determine if *Daubert* should be extended to "soft" sciences such as psychology and whether it can be applied to old scientific techniques that have already been accepted in court. For example, there have been challenges recently to fingerprint and handwriting testimony on the grounds that they have not been proven to be scientifically valid. There is little doubt that the effects of *Daubert* will continue to be felt for years to come. This type of challenge to already existing forms of scientific evidence could not have been mounted if the *Frye* general acceptance standard had been the yardstick of admissibility because this standard applies only to new and novel types of scientific evidence.

Laboratory reports

In almost any scientific endeavor, when experiments are performed, the results are recorded in a laboratory report. A complete and proper report should contain:

- An objective or purpose
- A list of materials and instruments used
- A detailed list of procedures and methods
- The results of the experiment or process, including all data produced

- A discussion of the results, including interpretation, statistical and other analyses, and known or possible sources of errors
- A detailed bibliography of all authoritative sources used in developing the experiments and interpreting the results.

A typical forensic science laboratory report does not meet the basic standards of a proper laboratory report. In many cases, a forensic science laboratory report contains only:

- Demographic data (name of suspect, submitting officer, location, agency, etc.)
- Unique number assigned to the case
- List of evidence received, with short descriptions
- Results of the analysis
- Signature of the analyst (sometimes notarized).

The evidentiary part of a typical laboratory report can be very brief; for example, a laboratory report for the analysis of a bag of marijuana might read: "*Received: one sealed plastic bag containing 25.3g of green-brown plant material. The green-brown plant material was identified as marijuana.*" Why do forensic scientists write such "unscientific" reports? First, one must consider the audience for a report from a crime laboratory. The report is generally written for police investigators, prosecutors, defense attorneys, and judges. One could argue that all these people need (or can understand) are the results of the analysis and the minimal laboratory report. Another, more cynical, reason is that providing a full report, with error rates, complete procedures, and supporting data, simply provides the adversarial party with ammunition with which to attack the scientists in court. On balance, however, full disclosure of laboratory examinations is desirable and necessary for justice to be served. Some people suggest that crime laboratories take their example from business reporting and write a complete report but include an executive summary for lawyers, police, and judges.

There is another interesting twist to laboratory reports: under certain conditions, the report can be a better "witness" than the scientist who wrote it. Over a year, a forensic scientist may perform thousands of examinations on hundreds or thousands of samples: it is not unusual for a drug chemist to analyze more than one hundred samples a month. Many of these are routine, involving cocaine, marijuana, heroin, and so on. Most of these cases will never be called to court and those that are may not be tried for many months or years. When an old case comes to trial, the scientist may not remember working on it. The only evidence that exists is the notes and report written at the time. In such situations, the best evidence of the analysis might be not the scientist, but their laboratory report.

Consider a forensic scientist, in court to testify in a case involving possession of cocaine. She analyzed this evidence eighteen months ago and has since analyzed hundreds of other cases involving cocaine and other types of drugs. At the time, she wrote a report detailing her findings and has the notes of her analysis. During direct examination, the prosecutor shows her a bag containing the drug evidence; he asks her if she can remember analyzing it. She answers that she cannot remember working on this specific bag of white powder. The prosecutor shows her the laboratory report she wrote, and he asks her if she can now remember working on this case. If the lab report triggers her memory, she can testify about the case. If she still cannot remember it, there is another route: if the scientist cannot remember doing the analysis even after looking at her report and her notes, she cannot testify but her report and notes can be admitted as proof of the analysis of the evidence. The report is clearly the most reliable evidence about the case. Only the original report and notes may be admitted: photocopies are not acceptable. This is the "best evidence" rule: it applies only to written materials.

Expert witnesses and testimony

Unlike lay witnesses, expert witnesses are often called upon to offer inferences or opinions based either on facts that they have observed or generated, or which are commonly relied upon by other experts in their field. This requires that the expert be qualified. The party (prosecution, plaintiff, or defense) that is offering the witness will establish their qualification to offer expert testimony and describe the field they are an expert in. The other side in the case has the opportunity to *voir dire* (a French phrase meaning "speak the truth") – to question – the witness on their qualifications. Formally, the court then rules that the witness will be permitted to testify as an expert in the described area (for example, illicit drugs or fingerprints). The court can refuse to allow a witness to testify as an expert but, as a matter of custom, seldom disqualifies one if both parties agree that they are suitable.

People often think experts must be university graduates, with an advanced degree such as a PhD. Although many experts do have PhDs or MDs, such education is not necessary to qualify as an expert. Rule 702 of the US Criminal Code defines an expert as "a witness qualified as an expert by knowledge, skill, experience, training, or education." A person can demonstrate expertise in a number of ways. Consider the following situation: an apartment building explodes, injuring several people. A short time before the explosion, some of the tenants had reported that they smelled gas. The main water heater in the building proves to have a leak. Did the old water heater fail? Did someone tamper with the gas line? Could there have been another cause for the gas explosion? Clearly, an expert on water heaters and gas systems would be needed. Most experts in this field learn their craft on the job, as apprentices. They may have a technical background, but no PhD would be needed: experience is the most important qualification. There would be no point in showing the water heater to the jury and asking them what caused the gas line to leak. The jury members have neither the knowledge and skills nor the aptitude to draw conclusions from the facts. The expert testimony in this case will be the opinion of the water-heater expert on what caused the gas leak.

The expert witness in court

Being an effective witness in court requires following certain guidelines about behavior and comportment. Some rules apply to all witnesses, whereas others are for expert witnesses only. Court testimony by any witness consists of direct examination by the party that has called them, followed by cross-examination by the other party. This may be followed by further direct examination and further cross-examination, until both parties have finished asking questions. In general, cross-examination must stay within the scope of the subject matter of the direct examination. Expert witnesses can consult their notes or reports but any documents they refer to in court can be inspected by either party.

Expert witnesses are often called upon to explain complicated scientific or technical matters, and it is easy for them to slip into the language or jargon of their trade. This language would be understood by other experts in the field but not by the average person. It is very important that expert witnesses explain difficult concepts using language that the average person can understand. A jury or judge is free to give whatever weight they choose to witnesses' testimony. Just because someone is agreed to be an expert doesn't mean the jury has to believe what they say. Expert witnesses are treated differently in court to non-expert (lay) witnesses. An expert must be qualified by the court every time they testify and the other party may challenge the expert's qualifications in the *voir dire*.

Scientific and technical evidence is treated differently than non-technical evidence in court, both because lay people find it difficult to understand and because it has an aura of reliability. The rules of evidence guide how and when evidence can be admitted. Laboratory reports of forensic scientific analysis can be important evidence in criminal and civil cases. They are the written record, along with the scientist's notes, of how the evidence was analyzed. If a witness cannot remember analyzing the evidence, the report itself may be the best witness.

This chapter has covered the forensic science system, the nature of evidence, its collection and analysis, and its presentation in court. The rest of the book discusses particular types of evidence. In a work this size, it is not possible to cover all types of forensic evidence and so only the most popular and commonly occurring will be discussed.

4

Forensic chemistry: illicit drugs

A **drug** can be defined as a substance that is designed to have specific effects, physical and/or emotional, on people or other animals. Most people think of drugs as something used to make us feel better: aspirin for a headache, antacids for heartburn, and so on. The vast majority of drugs are produced by pharmaceutical companies to treat a particular disease or disorder: these are **licit** drugs. (By the way, in this definition, ethyl alcohol, which we consume in beer, wine, and spirits, is not a drug in the US and many other countries. It may have some benefits in moderate quantities, but it is not usually taken for that purpose.)

Illicit drugs, sometimes called **controlled substances** or **abused drugs**, are of two types. The first is licit drugs that are abused or taken for purposes other than those for which they were originally developed. Methamphetamine is a good example: for many years, it was legitimately marketed as a stimulant, to counter feelings of fatigue or depression, and as an appetite suppressant. It played a role in controlling *hyperkinesia*, a disorder of the nervous system that manifests itself as hyperactivity. Today, however, methamphetamine is rarely used for these purposes; instead, large quantities of tablets and capsules stolen from legitimate channels and powdered forms made in illegal laboratories are taken to "get high." It is also possible to use a licit drug for the purpose it was developed, but fraudulently or inappropriately; for example, the use of steroids by athletes to give them an unfair competitive edge. The other type of illicit drug is a substance that has no recognized medical purpose. It can be a synthetic substance, such as phencyclidine (PCP), or it can be derived from a plant, like cocaine and morphine (which is then made into heroin). In some cases, part of the plant itself is ingested, such as marijuana or opium.

Because illicit drugs do not have any legitimate medical purpose, it is illegal to possess, use, grow, or sell them. Why? What harm is there in a person smoking marijuana in their home, not bothering anyone else? But many people believe this kind of wasteful, perhaps harmful, behavior does not improve society. In this chapter, we will discuss the two types of abused drugs, examine where they come from, discover a little of their history, and find out how they are used and how a forensic drug chemist goes about identifying them.

How abused drugs are controlled

In the UK, controlled drugs are those subject to the Misuse of Drugs Act of 1971. The Act places drugs in one of three categories: A, B, or C. The criterion used in placing a drug in a specific category is the amount of harm caused by its misuse: category A drugs are considered the most dangerous. Penalties for the use, sale, or manufacture of controlled drugs are tied to the categories, and therefore category A drugs carry the most severe penalties. There have been amendments to the 1971 Act, most notably in 1985 and in 2001. The latest regulations placed controlled drugs into one of five schedules. Drugs such as injectable amphetamines, cocaine (including crack), Ecstasy, heroin, and LSD are in category A. Powdered forms of amphetamines, barbiturates, and cannabis (marijuana) are in category B, although cannabis preparations were moved to category C between 2003 and 2009.

Category C includes many steroids, some sedatives, some mild amphetamines, and others.

In the US, the Uniform Controlled Substances Act defines controlled substances and assigns them to one of five Schedules. There are two criteria for placing drugs in a particular Schedule: potential for abuse, and the existence of a legitimate medical use as recognized by the Food and Drug Administration. Schedule I is reserved for those controlled substances with the highest potential for abuse and no acceptable medical use, such as LSD, heroin, Ecstasy, and PCP. Schedule II contains drugs that have a high potential for abuse but which also have a legitimate medical use, such as amphetamines, some barbiturates, cocaine, and narcotics such as morphine. Drugs in Schedules III to V have less potential for abuse and all have medical uses. Penalties for possession, distribution, and manufacture are tied to the Schedule, with the most severe penalties being for violations of drugs in Schedules I and II.

As well as the class or schedule to which a controlled drug belongs, there are other ways to classify these substances that are more organized and which put similar drugs in the same class. For example, we could classify drugs by their origin. In this system, all illicit drugs would fall into one of three classes: naturally occurring substances, such as marijuana, cocaine, or morphine; those derived from a naturally occurring substance, such as heroin, made from morphine, or LSD, made from lysergic acid; and synthetic substances such as methamphetamine, PCP, and oxycodone.

However, the most common method of classifying illicit drugs is by their major effects on a person. This is the system that we will use in this chapter. Under this scheme, there are four major classes of illicit drugs: stimulants, depressants, narcotics, and hallucinogens. We will discuss each of these classes and give a few common examples. It should be noted that there is a fifth class of illicit drugs, the performance-enhancing drugs, which includes many steroids, taken by athletes to improve their performance. This class of drugs will not be discussed in this book.

Central nervous system stimulants elevate a person's mood, temporarily increase energy levels, relieve some symptoms of depression, and stimulate people who are tired or lethargic. They are collectively called "uppers." For the most part, stimulants are not physically addictive but there are some exceptions. Many have powerful effects and can cause strong, intense psychological dependence. Two of the best examples of illicit stimulants are cocaine and methamphetamine.

The stimulant properties of cocaine have been known for centuries. It is a naturally occurring substance, derived from the plant *Erythroxylum coca.* (Note: not the same as the plant *Theobroma cacao*, from which chocolate is produced.) Coca grows mainly in one part of the world: the slopes of the Andes Mountains in South America. In recent times, the center of cocaine production has been in Colombia. Medically, cocaine is a topical anesthetic, causing numbness of any area of the body with which it comes into direct contact. It is still used as an anesthetic in some medical procedures but has largely been replaced by other drugs. For thousands of years, the indigenous farmers of the mountainous regions where coca is grown have known that they could increase their energy and endurance by chewing on the leaves of the coca plant. Cocaine is directly extracted from coca leaves, which are chopped up and dissolved in hot, alkaline water or an organic solvent. Then another solvent, containing hydrochloric acid, is added which removes and purifies the cocaine. The powder produced is *cocaine hydrochloride*, a flaky white powder that is sometimes called "snow" because it is so white and fluffy. It is also sometimes called "flake" or "blow". On the street, cocaine is seldom pure; typically, it is "cut," or diluted, with an inert powder such as sugar, so that the final product is 20–50% pure.

The most common way of taking this type of cocaine is by "snorting". A line of cocaine is laid down on a flat surface, such as a mirror. Then, using a tiny spoon or a straw, the cocaine is drawn up into the nose. The first sensation one gets from snorting cocaine is numbing of the nose and nasal passages (remember cocaine is a topical anesthetic). Within about thirty minutes, stimulation will follow and will last an hour or so, depending upon how much was snorted. Because the cocaine has to pass into the bloodstream to be effective, some of it is blocked and doesn't ever get through the nasal passages, thus reducing the potency of the drug. In the 1980s, a new form of cocaine – crack – became popular. Crack is prepared from cocaine hydrochloride using household chemicals such as lye and cleaning fluid. Unlike cocaine hydrochloride, which is a fluffy powder, crack comes in the form of small rocks, which are easily cracked or broken (hence the name). Also, unlike cocaine flake, crack is smoked, using a small pipe. In this form, cocaine can be physically addictive, because so much more of it gets into the bloodstream via the lungs. The US Federal Government and many states attach more severe penalties to the possession of crack than they do to the same amount of cocaine hydrochloride. (At the time of writing, the US Congress has passed legislation that reduces the disparity in penalties for possession of crack and cocaine.)

Methamphetamine and amphetamine have been popular illicit drugs for more than forty years. Methamphetamine is relatively easy to produce: there are many small laboratories in homes, motel rooms, and even cars. In some places in the US, meth labs are almost an epidemic. Methamphetamine was nicknamed "speed" on the streets, because of its powerful stimulant properties, especially when taken pure. High doses of this drug can cause death and, in the 1960s, the warning on the street was that "speed kills." A popular method of preparation of methamphetamine uses an over-the-counter cold remedy, *pseudoephedrine*, a very popular decongestant. Some people buy huge quantities of cold remedies and extract the pseudoephedrine to make methamphetamine. The other major ingredient needed for this method of preparation of methamphetamine is ammonia. Many farmers use pure, liquid, anhydrous ammonia as an ingredient in fertilizer and keep huge tanks of it on their property. Reports of thefts of large quantities of ammonia are rising all over the country.

In the 1960s and 1970s, depressants were much more popular illicit drugs than they are today. By far the most popular depressants were barbiturates; a family of drugs prescribed to relieve anxiety, nervousness, and restlessness. Barbiturates range from the very mild, such as phenobarbital, which was at one time an ingredient of some allergy medicines, to the very powerful, such as pentobarbital and thiopental barbiturate. The former is used to put very sick animals to sleep and has been used as the "lethal injection" for some convicted criminals. Thiopental barbiturate, or sodium pentothal, is used as a general anesthetic during major surgery.

The most notorious of the illicit drugs are the hallucinogens. These drugs cause hallucinations, which means they cause people to see and hear things that aren't there. Marijuana has been called by many colorful names over the hundreds of years that it has been used, including "weed", "hop", "Mary Jane", "toke", and hundreds of others. Marijuana is classified as a hallucinogen largely because it doesn't fit in any other categories; it doesn't cause hallucinations to the same degree as do other members of this group, for example LSD, some mushrooms, and some cactus extracts. Its effects are usually more of a "mellowing out" but can be wide ranging, depending upon the person and how experienced they are with the drug. In many people, marijuana stimulates appetite and users report ravenous hunger after smoking it. Marijuana belongs to the genus *Cannabis*. It grows almost anywhere, but favors warm and sunny conditions. The leaves and flowers of the plant contain a number of substances that cause the psychological effects of marijuana. The most important member of this group of chemicals has the tongue-twisting name of tetrahydrocannabinol (THC). Most commonly, the leaves and flowering parts are separated from the plant and dried in an oven. Then they are chopped, rolled into cigarettes, and smoked. The higher the THC content, the more potent the effects: marijuana cigarettes range upwards from 1% THC, but genetically engineered marijuana, with a THC content of nearly 40%, has been reported! The stems, roots, and seeds do not contain appreciable quantities of THC and are thus not controlled in most US states. There are also a number of preparations of marijuana. Sometimes, the pure resin is harvested from the flowering parts. This thick, sticky liquid, called "hashish oil" or "hash oil", has the highest THC content of any part of the plant. It is smoked in small pipes designed for the purpose. It is also common to take chopped-up marijuana and extract it with a solvent. When the solvent is evaporated, a semi-solid, cake-like form of hashish remains. This is formed into bricks and sold. To use it, a small piece is broken off and smoked in a hash pipe or "bong." Sometimes marijuana leaves are mixed with or coated with another drug, such as PCP: this is called "wobble weed." Figure 2 shows some marijuana paraphernalia.

In recent years, some medical research has shown that marijuana may have some benefits in treating certain afflictions. For

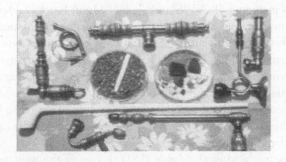

Figure 2 Drug paraphernalia used in smoking marijuana

example, marijuana has been used to treat glaucoma, a progressive eye disease that eventually leads to blindness. There is some evidence that marijuana may stop the progress of the disease, although it doesn't reverse it. With certain cancers, the patient is treated with powerful drugs that seek to arrest the progress of the disease (chemotherapy). These drugs can destroy cancer cells but they have serious side effects such as hair loss and extreme nausea. There is some evidence that marijuana may relieve the nausea symptoms for a short time. In the past few years, a number of states in the US have adopted medical marijuana laws that permit controlled use of marijuana for certain diseases. In these cases, a physician has to certify the need for the drug and it has to be approved by a court.

Two US states, Colorado and Washington, have recently legalized the sale and use of small quantities of marijuana. A few other states are waiting to see how this works out with an eye to also legalizing marijuana.

Another recent development in marijuana use and abuse is the appearance of so-called **synthetic marijuana**. The generic term "spice" has been used to describe a wide variety of herbal concoctions that are purported to produce similar psychoactive effects as marijuana and are marketed as safe and legal alternatives. Spice is being marketed under a bewildering variety of names including "K2," "Skunk," and "Moon Rocks." Many of these preparations are labeled "not for human consumption" in an effort to circumvent liability and FDA regulations. Synthetic marijuana products generally contain shredded plant material and synthetic cannabinoid compounds. Because of their high potential for abuse, the most common of these compounds are in Schedule I and possession is illegal. The producers try to stay a step ahead of law enforcement by continually varying the cannabinoid compounds used.

Lysergic acid diethylamide (LSD) is one of the most potent hallucinogens. One small drop can cause visual and auditory hallucinations lasting up to twelve hours. Because of its potency, it is taken in some odd forms. The most common is "blotter acid," in which the LSD is diluted with a solvent and impregnated on to absorbent paper, which is cut into tiny squares and eaten. LSD is also made into tiny tablets, or "microdots," with colorful names such as "orange sunshine" or "purple haze." It can be mixed with gelatin and cut into small squares called "window panes." It has even been found on decals, similar to those that children lick and put on their bodies. Since LSD can be absorbed through the skin, these tattoos can cause an hallucinogenic episode. Figure 3 shows some blotter acid LSD.

The term **narcotic** is often associated with illicit drugs, and generally has a bad reputation in the US. It comes from the Greek root "*narco*" meaning "sleep" – one of the major effects of all narcotics is that they cause sleep. Strictly speaking, "narcotic" refers to substances that are derived from the opium poppy, *Papaver somniferum*. Remember *The Wizard of Oz*, where Dorothy and her friends fall asleep while tramping through the poppy fields? The seedpod of the poppy plant contains a gooey resin; for centuries people smoked this dried resin in opium dens. About 10% of this resin is morphine (named for

Figure 3 Blotter acid. LSD is diluted in alcohol and then poured onto absorbent paper. The paper is then cut into squares and eaten. A square is one dose

Morpheus, the Greek god of sleep), a powerful narcotic. As well as causing sleep, morphine exhibits the other major characteristic of narcotics: it relieves pain. Morphine is used as pain relief for people who have had major surgery or trauma. Codeine is another naturally occurring narcotic, less powerful than morphine. It is mainly used for treating coughs; it puts the cough centers "to sleep." It is also mixed with over-the-counter analgesics, such as acetaminophen, for treatment of pain after minor surgery. Other narcotics occur in opium in trace quantities.

The most famous (or infamous) narcotic is heroin. Heroin is a synthetic substance made from morphine. Opium poppies mainly grow in the Far East; in a typical synthesis route, the raw opium is shipped to France, where the morphine is extracted and converted to heroin, which is shipped worldwide. The movie *The French Connection* tells the story of this drug trade. Heroin is ten times stronger than morphine and is used in some countries for the same purposes as morphine. In the US, heroin has no accepted medical use and is in Federal Schedule I. All narcotics are physically addictive, but heroin is especially so; its withdrawal symptoms can be quite severe, but are seldom fatal.

Heroin is sold on the street as a white or brown powder that contains about 5% heroin; the rest is cutting agents, such as sugars. It is commonly ingested by injection, which can cause problems beyond the heroin itself. Addicts habitually share needles, which is a good way to transmit blood-borne diseases such as AIDS and hepatitis. Typically, some of the powder is put in a small container, such as a discarded bottle cap, and some water added. The mixture is heated to dissolve the heroin and then the liquid is pulled into the syringe, filtered through a small wad of cotton or similar material. Heroin addicts have telltale needle marks on their arms, and will often find other places on their bodies to inject the drug, such as between the toes.

In recent years, many synthetic narcotics have been developed. These have similar properties to some of the naturally

occurring ones, but fewer side effects. The best known is metha-
done, which is used as a substitute for heroin for people who are
trying to "kick the habit." In the past decade or so, oxycodone
has returned to the scene as a "rave" drug, seen at wild parties
where lots of drugs and alcohol are used.

Analysis of illicit drugs

Agents of the US Drug Enforcement Administration, as well as
personnel of the state and local police, are dedicated to reducing
the flow of drugs into the US and arresting people who sell them
to others or possess large quantities. When drugs are seized they
are sent to a crime laboratory for analysis by forensic drug chemists. A number of considerations determine how the drugs will
be analyzed, including:

* What the drug is and what form it is in
* Whether there is a large amount of the drug in one package
  or in many packages
* Whether there is a very small amount of the drug
* What the weight of the drug mixture is.

Any conclusion given by a forensic scientist in a court or on a
laboratory report must be scientifically reliable and defendable.
If a scientist identifies a white powder as containing cocaine,
they must prove this *to a degree of reasonable scientific certainty*. This
is the standard of proof in a court. There must be no reasonable alternative to the conclusion reached by the scientist. For
this reason, most drug samples must have at least one confirmatory test performed. In general, tests for drugs proceed from the
general to the specific. Each test serves to give more information
about the possible identity of the drug and either the scheme as a
whole or a confirmatory test will positively identify the drug.

The most general tests for drugs are the screening tests, sometimes called spot tests or field tests. There are screening tests

for most of the common illicit drugs, which usually consist of adding one or more chemical reagents to a sample of the drug and observing any color changes. For example, the common screening test for marijuana involves three chemicals, and the final color is purple; the test for cocaine uses three chemicals and the final color is turquoise. The purpose of these tests is to narrow down the possibilities when seeking to identify a drug, which can be especially important if the submitted sample is a white powder. A white powder could be any one of a number of things and screening tests can be very important in leading the chemist towards the proper identification. It is important to emphasize that screening tests are never used to confirm the presence of a specific drug; for each screening test, there may be many substances that could give a positive reaction.

Very few illicit drugs, especially powders, are sold on the street in a pure form; almost all of them are diluted with one or more cutting agents. To positively identify the drug, it must be separated from the cutting agents. This can be done on a large scale using liquid solvents to extract the drug. On a small scale, where only a small amount of the drug may be present, instrumental techniques, such as gas or liquid chromatography, are used. Most drug samples must be confirmed by a single test, so that there is no uncertainty as to the identity of the drug. In most crime laboratories, the confirmatory test uses the technique of mass spectrometry, in which molecules of the drug are ionized and sorted according to their mass. The results are displayed as a pattern, unique to a particular substance: cocaine will form a particular pattern of ion fragments that is different than the pattern for heroin or any other substance in the world. Mass spectrometry is a very good confirmatory test for cocaine.

One of the few drugs that doesn't normally require a confirmatory test is marijuana, because it is an easily recognized plant. The visual recognition of the plant is a major part of the testing scheme. Other tests, such as a screening test and perhaps a separation test to isolate the THC, are usually performed and the scheme as a whole considered confirmatory for marijuana.

Sometimes it is not possible to confirm the presence of a drug, perhaps when there is so little of the drug present that there is not enough to do all the necessary tests, for example when testing the residue in a syringe for heroin or the dust in a straw for cocaine. In such cases, a qualified opinion of the identity of the drug may have to be given. Sometimes the opposite situation arises, when there is a very large amount of the drug in many packages; decisions must be made as to how the packages will be sampled and tested. I once had a case involving 16,000 pounds of marijuana in 50-pound bricks; samples from each of the 320 bricks were tested. In another case, I received 535 small packets suspected to contain cocaine. All were opened, weighed, and screened; they were all about the same weight and responded the same to screening tests. A portion of the packets were subject to further testing, to confirm the presence of cocaine. Such sampling is permissible, as long as representative samples are tested.

Forensic toxicology

Thus far, this chapter has discussed illicit drugs and how they are encountered on the street. The question of why people abuse these drugs is partially answered by the concept of *potential for abuse*: people take these drugs because doing so makes them feel good. They become more awake and alert, or are able to calm down and decrease anxiety, or are able to experience hallucinations. We now turn our attention to what happens to drugs, physically and chemically, when they are ingested. Some drugs have pleasurable or therapeutic effects when taken in proper amounts but many have harmful or fatal side effects when abused. The remainder of this chapter will center on the fate of drugs once they have been ingested.

Toxicology is a part of the science of pharmacology; the study of drugs and their harmful and beneficial effects on living things. When scientists use the principles of pharmacology to analyze the harmful effects of drugs and poisons on living things in cases involving the criminal justice system, they are practicing forensic toxicology. The part of pharmacology that we will concentrate on is pharmacodynamics, the fate of a drug when ingested.

Drugs can be administered in a number of ways: swallowing a powder, tablet, or capsule; dissolving a powder in water and drinking it; inhaling a liquid or vapor through the nose; via an intramuscular, subcutaneous, or intravenous injection with a syringe and needle; or smoked. The best method of ingestion for a particular drug depends upon how it interacts with organs such as the stomach; for example, if a drug is destroyed by stomach acids, it cannot be taken by mouth. To prevent a drug from dissolving too quickly in the stomach or small intestine, it may be coated with a slow-dissolving material or be produced in the form of tiny, coated particles that enter the bloodstream over a long period of time (timed-release capsules).

The route of ingestion also affects the rate at which the drug enters the bloodstream; this has a profound influence upon the effects of the drug. Intravenous injections (directly into the bloodstream) provide the fastest route, followed by intramuscular and subcutaneous injections. Oral administration is normally the slowest means of getting a drug into the bloodstream. If a drug is taken orally, it will first enter the stomach. It may then pass from the stomach, through the pylorus (a valve that connects the stomach to the small intestine), into the small intestine. Some drugs are absorbed into the bloodstream from the stomach, some from the small intestine and some from both. With the exception of oral ingestion, the drug user has no control over the rate of absorption of a drug. When a drug is taken orally, the rate of absorption depends upon what is in the stomach. If the stomach is empty, the drug will be absorbed rapidly. If there is food in the stomach, the drug will have to compete with the food for absorption into the bloodstream, which means the drug will be absorbed more slowly and the ultimate concentration of the drug in the blood will be lower than if the stomach were empty. Once drugs enter the bloodstream, they circulate throughout the body. Although some drugs are targeted at specific organs, such as the heart, drugs have their most important effects on the brain. Pharmaceutical chemistry has advanced to the point where drugs can be designed to have a particular interaction with a particular part of the brain, resulting in a predictable effect.

The higher the concentration of the drug in the bloodstream, the more pronounced its effects will be. Certain effects don't even occur at low drug concentrations. In theory, every drug should be distributed more or less equally throughout the body, because the bloodstream carries the drug to every tissue but, in fact, some drugs tend to collect in certain tissues or organs – for example, pesticides collect and build up in fatty tissues. A pesticide may not cause too much harm at low concentration but, as it builds up in fatty tissues rather than being eliminated, its concentration can reach toxic levels over time. Heavy metals, such as mercury or lead, collect preferentially in teeth and gums, finger- and toenails, and hair. LSD and marijuana appear to collect and remain in certain parts of the brain, which may explain the so-called "flashbacks" that occur with LSD use, when a person can have a relapse from LSD taken years earlier.

After reaching a maximum, the concentration of a drug in the body will begin to decrease. Pharmacologists use the term **half-life** for drugs; this is the time it takes for the concentration of a drug to drop to half. Half-lives vary greatly: the hypnotic drug GHB has a half-life of about thirty minutes, whereas cocaine's half-life is sixty to ninety minutes. By contrast, heroin has a half-life of only three minutes! The decrease in concentration of a drug is caused by two processes: metabolism and elimination. As drugs circulate throughout the body, sooner or later they reach the liver. The liver has the ability to change a drug into a different substance, or **metabolite**. This primary metabolite may be metabolized into another substance, the secondary metabolite. For example, the primary metabolite of heroin is morphine, another naturally occurring narcotic. Metabolism in the liver generally accomplishes one of two things: it changes the drug into a less harmful (less toxic) substance or into a form that makes it easier to eliminate in the urine, normally by changing the drug into an ionic form, or salt, that is much more soluble in water, the main component of urine. With many drugs, metabolism takes place so quickly that toxicologists don't look for the parent drug in a blood sample; they look instead for known metabolites whose presence proves that the parent drug was previously there.

There are several ways drugs can be eliminated from the body. If the drug is volatile (easily vaporized), it can be exhaled in the breath. If the drug is water-soluble, it can be sweated out during vigorous exercise or exposure to hot, humid conditions. At best, these methods account for only a small percentage of the elimination of drugs. The majority of drugs are eliminated in urine, either as the drug itself or after metabolism by the liver. The process is entirely under the control of the liver and kidneys. The person has no influence over the rate at which this happens: no intervention can speed it up or slow it down. There have been a number of high-profile cases involving entertainers who accidentally overdosed on alcohol and barbiturates. Neither substance was ingested at a high enough concentration to cause death: it was the combination of the two that killed. This phenomenon, whereby someone exhibits magnified effects from a combination of drugs, is called **synergism**: a term used in a large number of applications from drugs to business, meaning "the whole is greater than the sum of the parts." In the overdose cases, the effects of the alcohol and barbiturates taken together were greater than the sum of their effects would have been if taken separately. Both alcohol and barbiturates are central nervous system depressants; their synergistic effects slowed down the victim's respiration so much that they stopped breathing and died. Synergism can be very tricky: with so many new drugs coming on the market, it is very important for pharmaceutical companies to test new drugs against existing ones to uncover possibly dangerous synergisms. Toxicologists and pathologists must be careful in assessing the role that drugs could have had in causing death. Synergism must be ruled out before drug levels are taken into account when determining the cause and manner of death.

Tolerance of a drug occurs when increasing doses are required for the same level of effect. It shows up very often in people who continually abuse the same drug. For example, someone who abuses methamphetamine for the first time may get "high" from a 10mg dose; after several days they might find they must take 20mg at a time to get the same effects. Then it takes 30mg, and so on. This can become a serious problem when the person becomes addicted to a drug and wants to quit. If they try to quit, withdrawal symptoms will set in because they have become physically dependent on the drug. In some cases, such as barbiturates, sudden ("cold turkey") withdrawal can be fatal, so the person has to be taken off the drug very slowly. If a person becomes tolerant to a drug, that means they can tolerate ever-larger quantities without dangerous reactions. When a person dies and a high concentration of a drug is found in their bloodstream, the toxicologist has to find out the drug history of that person before making a conclusion about the role that the drug played in their death. A high concentration does not necessarily mean that the drug caused their death or even contributed to it.

In certain drugs, a type of reverse tolerance has been noted. This is sometimes reported by marijuana users, who say that they get more heightened effects over time without taking more of the drug. One explanation is that the symptoms resulting from marijuana use are learned behavior: the more one smokes marijuana, the more its effects will be expected and this is perceived as reverse tolerance. There is also evidence that THC, the active ingredient in marijuana, may remain in the body for months after ingestion and, with regular use, will increase in concentration, thus increasing its effects. LSD is another drug to which reverse tolerance has been reported. The reasons for this are not well understood.

Workplace drug testing

In recent years, government and private employers worldwide have put increased emphasis on identifying employees who use illicit (and some licit) drugs while working. Workplace drug use costs millions in lost productivity, decreased safety, increased death, and injuries. In many workplaces, employees are tested for drugs before they begin work and then periodically in random, unannounced tests. In this final section of the chapter, we will discuss some of the major issues in workplace drug testing.

Most workplace drug testing is performed on urine samples. The use of urine raises issues of possible contamination or adulteration. Some workers, in an effort to avoid detection, smuggle in drug-free urine; others attempt to dilute a sample of urine with water to reduce drug concentrations below thresholds (more about this later). Some people take diuretic drugs before a drug test to flush their system (diuretics cause more frequent urination).

Personnel at the clinics or offices where samples are collected are not necessarily familiar with the concept of "chain of custody" and security requirements, which can result in mishandled, lost, or contaminated samples. For example, if the urine sample is not covered tightly, water may evaporate, increasing the concentrations of all dissolved materials, including drugs. In a crime laboratory, there are generally accepted schemes for the analysis of illicit and licit drugs and clinical laboratories have consensus protocols for analysis of drugs that have been ingested. Often, these two types of protocols are different. For example, if a patient has taken a drug and the hospital wishes to monitor its level, there is no need for confirmation: the analyst already knows what drug has been taken. In forensics, the identity of drugs is *always* confirmed using mass spectrometry. If a clinical laboratory analyzes urine for drugs and notes the presence of cocaine, they may not do a confirmatory test because they do not normally do so. As a result, should the case get to court, the analysis of the drug may not be admissible or may be thrown out because it is inadequate.

All laboratories use preliminary or screening tests for urine drug testing. These tests usually screen for a battery of illicit drugs, including marijuana, cocaine, heroin, and methamphetamine; other drugs may be included in the screen if requested by the employer. These preliminary tests determine presumptively if a drug is present. All tests have limits of detection, below which a drug cannot be detected even if it is present. No employer should ever take action against an employee solely on the basis of a presumptive positive test. These tests are not specific; many will cross-react to a legal substance that is similar to an illicit drug. For example, some preliminary tests respond the same way to methamphetamine and pseudoephedrine, a legal, over-the-counter, allergy medicine. For this reason, all preliminary drug tests should be confirmed.

In recent years, the technique of using hair to test for drugs has matured. Almost all drugs that are tested for in urine can also be tested for in hair. Hair testing overcomes the sampling issues that occur with urine; only a few hairs are needed to test for most drugs and taking samples is less invasive. Hair is not subject to contamination from passive inhalation of or exposure to marijuana cigarette smoke. It is more expensive than urine testing but prices have come down recently. The major advantage of hair testing is that the hair contains drug residues for every time a drug has been taken as long as the hair has been present, which is often many months. Thus, hair analysis for drugs gives a drug history rather than just the snapshot of drug use provided by a urine test.

Illicit drugs represent nearly half of the forensic cases received by crime laboratories in the US; similar amounts are being analyzed worldwide. There are four major classes of illicit drugs; stimulants, depressants, narcotics, and hallucinogens. Recently, some performance-enhancing drugs have made up a fifth class. In the UK and US, controlled drugs are classed in various schedules according to their medical uses and potential for abuse. Drugs can be naturally occurring, semi-synthetic or totally synthetic. The form of the drug often dictates how it will be analyzed. Methods of analysis include preliminary screening tests, separation tests, and confirmation tests. Forensic toxicology is the science of the analysis of illicit and licit drugs that may be used in a forensic case and is concerned with the fate of drugs once they are ingested. The ultimate effects of drugs depend upon their concentrations in the brain and bloodstream. This, in turn, depends upon their rate of absorption into and elimination from the body. These rates vary from drug to drug and person to person.

Drug evidence is probably the best developed in terms of its analytical schemes and the understanding of attorneys and judges. Drugs are easily identified but it is usually not possible to associate a sample of drugs with a larger source, and few laboratories even attempt this type of association.

The following three chapters in the book venture further into the area of forensic chemistry, in which the methods and techniques of chemistry are employed to identify and characterize chemical and trace evidence, to provide some degree of association with a particular source. In some of these areas, the characteristics of transfer of evidence from one place to another, and its persistence once it has been transferred, can be as important as the chemical and physical nature of the evidence itself.

5

Forensic chemistry: fires and explosions

On April 19, 1995, a truck containing hundreds of pounds of ammonium nitrate mixed with fuel oil (ANFO) was parked outside the Alfred P. Murrah Federal Building in Oklahoma City, Oklahoma. The explosives in the truck were detonated. The building was almost completely destroyed and the concussion caused windows to break in buildings several blocks away. Hundreds of people were killed. The explosive used in the Murrah building bombing was made from readily available chemicals: ammonium nitrate is a common commercial fertilizer, sold in large bags in pellet form; fuel oil, commonly used to heat homes and commercial buildings, is available in containers of every size from bottles to tanks. The mixture of ammonium nitrate pellets saturated with fuel oil contains everything needed to cause a powerful explosion except the initiator; in the Oklahoma City bombing, this came from a spark set off by an electrical timing device.

On December 4, 1979, a fire broke out in a dwelling in East Yorkshire, England. The residents of the home, Edith Hastie and her four sons, were asleep at the time. One of the sons rescued his mother by pushing her out of an upstairs window. That son and two of the other sons perished as a result of the fire. One son survived by escaping through a window in a back bedroom, where the fire was less intense. Hastie's husband was in prison at the time and her three daughters were else-where during the fire. The Hastie family was not popular in the neighborhood where they lived, as the sons were often accused of committing petty crimes in the area. With this informa-tion, the arson investigators began to focus on someone in the neighborhood who might have been seeking revenge. A teen-ager, Bruce Lee, who was living in the area, confessed to the police that he set the letterbox afire in revenge against one of the sons with whom he had some run-ins and sexual contact. Lee had also had designs on one of the Hastie daughters but had been rebuffed. Lee ultimately confessed to starting not only the Hastie fire but also nine others in the same area. He was ultimately convicted of twenty-six counts of manslaughter (reduced from murder on the grounds of diminished responsi-bility) and of eleven counts of arson.

In this chapter, we shall examine fires and explosions and see how they are similar in many ways, yet different in important respects. We shall also see how fire and explosion scenes are searched and what evidence is recovered and analyzed.

Combustion

Fires and explosions are really all caused by the same chemi-cal reaction: **combustion**, the reaction of a fuel with oxygen. Complete combustion results in the formation of oxides (chemi-cal compounds containing oxygen) and water, and in the evolu-tion of energy. Incomplete combustion forms the same products (and others) and also evolves energy, but not as much. Chemical reactions that evolve energy are **exothermic**. Not all oxidation reactions are exothermic: for example, the slow reaction of iron with oxygen to form rust (iron oxide) is not; but then, iron is not a fuel. Reactions of fuels with oxygen are always exothermic and the energy is produced as light and heat. One of the most familiar fuels is gasoline (petrol), which is distilled from petroleum (crude oil). Gasoline contains more than three hundred substances, mostly hydrocarbons (different compounds of carbon and hydrogen). Hydrocarbons are potent fuels that react with oxygen to give off lots of energy.

In an internal combustion (automobile) engine, the gasoline and air are confined in a small space, the combustion chamber; a spark from a spark plug provides the energy that starts the combustion. The energy evolved by the combustion heats up the products of the reaction, converting them to vapor. These hot, rapidly expanding gases push the pistons and cause the car to move. This combustion appears to be an explosion but is actually a fire: it's the confinement of the reaction that makes it look like an explosion. Real explosions are also combustion reactions: the difference between a fire and an explosion is the amount of energy produced by the combustion and how this energy interacts with the products of the reaction. As we shall see, explosives are differentiated by the velocity of the gases that escape from the combustion. The amount of energy produced by a combustion reaction depends in part on how intimately the fuel and the oxygen are mixed. The closer together the oxygen atoms and the fuel atoms, the more energy will be produced and the higher will be the velocity of the escaping gases.

Fires

Fires can cause horrific damage, both to structures and people. Crowded nightclubs seem to be the location of some of the world's most deadly fires; for example, on November 30, 2002, a fire in a nightclub in Caracas, Venezuela, killed forty-seven people. Its cause was never determined but was believed to be either faulty wiring or a kitchen fire. When many people think of fires, they think of arson, fires that are deliberately started with the intent to cause damage or kill, but some of the world's most notorious fires have been started accidentally.

What is arson? How is the cause of a fire determined? What role does a crime laboratory play in fire investigation? Fires are the result of a combustion reaction; the energy released by the reaction causes the fuel to burn and we see the familiar orange flames and smoke. Three things are necessary for combustion: fuel, oxygen, and enough heat (activation energy) to get the fire started and keep it burning. Fire experts speak of the **fire triangle** as a shorthand way of describing the components: see Figure 4. The combustion reactions that produce fires are considered slow: typical fuels, such as wood, plastic, gasoline, and so on, do not yield enough energy to produce explosions and the oxygen needed comes mainly from the air surrounding the fire, which, on a chemical scale, is too far away from the fuel for rapid combustion. The fuel must be vaporized and the oxygen molecules broken into atoms, also a slow process. The result is flames and hot gases with a relatively slow escape velocity.

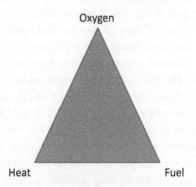

Figure 4 The fire triangle. All three elements need to be present to start and sustain a fire

The fire triangle shows how fires might be suppressed and how fire extinguishers operate. Since all three elements of the fire triangle must be present to sustain a fire, depriving the fire of just one element will extinguish it. For example, if the temperature of the fire drops to the point where the fuel is not vaporized, the fire will go out; liquid or solid fuels do not burn easily. Water is used to douse many types of fires because it cools them down to this point. Although widely used, water is not a universal fire extinguisher; it should not be used on electrical fires, because it conducts electricity and so may spread the fire rather than extinguishing it. If the oxygen is removed from a fire, even for a short time, the fire will go out. This is the principle behind extinguishing a candle, which is, of course, a controlled fire: even though blowing on the candle may introduce more oxygen, it is traveling too fast past the wick to support combustion. Carbon dioxide fire extinguishers replace the oxygen surrounding the fire with carbon dioxide, which cannot support combustion. Another way to deprive a fire of oxygen is to smother it: small fires can be extinguished by covering them with blankets, and larger fires can be doused by foam fire extinguishers, in which the non-flammable foam separates the fuel from the oxygen. Foam extinguishers are often used to control fires caused by fuel spills in gas stations or on airport runways. Water is not effective as an extinguisher in such fires, because water and most fuels don't mix and the water disperses the fire rather than extinguishing it.

There are three causes of fires: natural, accidental, and deliberate. An example of a natural fire would be one caused by lightning; an accidental fire would be one caused by an unintended electrical appliance overload or a malfunctioning furnace. Of course, not all electrical overloads or malfunctioning furnaces are accidental fires. Deliberate fires are also called **incendiary** fires. Not all incendiary fires are arson: if you set fire to a pile of leaves in the fall, you have started an incendiary fire but your intent is not to burn down your home or commit some other crime, so the fire is not arson. The cause of a fire is determined in an investigation conducted by a fire scene investigator, trained to identify clues that point to the cause. Such investigations can be summed up as the search to find a natural or accidental cause; if these can be eliminated, the fire must be deliberate.

Investigating fires

Investigating a fire can be a difficult, dangerous, tedious process. When the investigator arrives at the scene, the fire has normally been put out. Hundreds or thousands of gallons of water will have soaked everything in the building. The electricity and gas will generally be turned off to avoid further danger. The floors and walls (especially if made of a material such as wood) may have been weakened by the fire and could be in danger of collapsing under the weight. If the fire has been particularly destructive, the higher levels of the building may have collapsed, piling tons of debris onto the lower levels.

The key to determining the cause of the fire is to find its point of origin; the location where the fire started. If the fire is accidental, as with a malfunctioning appliance, the point of origin will be by the appliance; if someone went to sleep on a couch smoking a cigarette, the couch would be the point of origin. If the fire were started deliberately, perhaps using gasoline, the point of origin would be where the gasoline was poured. Fires generally burn upwards; flames and hot escaping gases are less dense than air at room temperature and tend to rise, carrying the heat produced by the fire. Deliberately set fires are likely to be started on a lower level of a building, because arsonists know that fires travel upwards and they want to cause maximum damage: they also don't want to be caught on a higher floor of the building when the fire starts, which may block their exit. Severe damage to a structure may cause the upper floors to collapse onto lower floors, piling debris over the point of origin, which must be carefully removed, layer by layer, often in a dark, wet environment.

A number of clues can point to the point of origin but they are not always reliable and can mislead the fire scene investigator. The point of origin is often the site of the most intense burning, and the fire tends to spread up and out from there, forming characteristic "V-shaped" burn patterns. These patterns will be seen elsewhere if secondary fires have started. Intense burning at the point of origin may cause concrete to spall (fragment), blister, or crack, or cause glass to crack in characteristic ways.

If an appliance such as a furnace is the point of origin, it will be necessary to determine if it failed or malfunctioned and if such failure were deliberate or accidental. As you can imagine, this is not always easy, given the extensive damage the appliance may have suffered. The fire scene investigator may call in other experts, such as a heating contractor, to examine a furnace, but often it is not possible to determine the nature of the involvement of the appliance.

Fuels generally do not burn while they are solids and liquids but must first be vaporized: this means that there must be sufficient heat to cause vaporization. This may not be too difficult with fuels such as paper or cloth, but can be quite problematic with chunks of wood, tile flooring, wall materials, and so on. One way to speed up a fire or cause materials to burn that otherwise would not is to use an accelerant, a liquid fuel that burns easily and supplies the energy needed to vaporize other materials. By far the most common accelerant is gasoline but charcoal lighters, paint thinners, and camp stove fuels are also used. Accelerants may be detected in a number of ways: there may be intense burning or a fire trail at the scene, or accelerant "sniffing" instruments can be used to detect very small amounts of hydrocarbons such as gasoline. Among the most sensitive accelerant detectors are trained dogs, which can sniff out a fire scene and hit on possible hydrocarbon fuels with great sensitivity and accuracy. Large fire departments use "fire dogs" in their investigations unit.

The first step in determining if a fire is incendiary is to eliminate all natural and accidental causes. Finding the point of origin of the fire is crucial: a number of clues, some better than others, can indicate that a fire was set on purpose. The final determination of the nature of the fire is the responsibility of the fire scene investigator, who considers all the evidence, including clues other than the physical evidence of the fire. Some of the more common indicators of an incendiary fire are:

- The presence of an accelerant: A splash pattern at the point of origin is often indicative of the presence of an accelerant. If the proper evidence is collected and preserved, a forensic chemist can identify the type of accelerant. Since accelerants give off large amounts of heat, their presence is also signaled by intense, localized heat damage. However, the investigator has to be careful in making conclusions from accelerant burn patterns – many people store gasoline, lamp oil, or other fuels in their homes, and, if a fire spreads to a container of one of these materials, it will probably burn. Thus, accelerants may be present even at accidental or natural fires.

- Fire trail: One way to quickly involve several areas of a building in a fire is to spread an accelerant from one place to another by pouring it in a trail. The fire will follow the trail and involve many locations at once. A fire trail is highly indicative of an incendiary fire.

- Multiple points of origin: Another way of rapidly spreading a fire is to set up several points of origin and ignite the fires simultaneously. This is almost always an indicator of arson. The one notable exception is where an electrical overload or short occurs in the walls of a building, which can spread throughout the wiring to several locations and set off fires in many places at once.

- Copious amounts of black, sooty smoke: This may be evidence of burning of a hydrocarbon fuel such as gasoline or oil. Large amounts of smoke indicate a lot of fuel, which may indicate an incendiary fire.

If the fire scene investigator suspects arson and locates the point of origin or a fire trail, debris from the fire can be collected and sent for analysis. Fire debris must be packed in an airtight container, to minimize evaporation of any accelerant (unused paint cans are the preferred containers). The major task of the laboratory is to isolate accelerant residues from the debris and identify them. Gentle heating of the debris container will vaporize some of the accelerant, which can be withdrawn using a gas-tight syringe and analyzed by gas chromatography. The fire scene investigator will use this evidence when drawing conclusions about the nature of the fire. The mere presence of an accelerant, especially a common one such as gasoline, is not proof that the fire was incendiary; likewise, the absence of an accelerant does not rule out arson. An accelerant may not have been used, too much of it burned in the fire to recover identifiable residues, or the wrong evidence may have been recovered.

Explosions

An explosion is like a fire, only more powerful. Sometimes a fire can appear to be an explosion. If a fuel, such as gasoline, is confined to a closed space and set on fire, the gases produced will cause pressure to build up until the container ruptures. Most people would refer to this as an explosion, but it is also just a confined fire. To someone standing nearby, this is a distinction without a difference: it sure looks like an explosion. Most people think of an explosion as a violent release of energy but a confined fire can also fit this definition. When a gun is fired, it looks like there has been an explosion inside the cartridge that expels the bullet, but this is also a confined fire because smokeless powder (the propellant) burns rather than explodes.

For a forensic chemist, however, there are important differences between a confined fire and an explosion.

Explosion v. fire

Unlike nuclear explosions, chemical explosions are combustions just like fires. The difference is in how much energy is emitted by a given amount of fuel and how intimately the oxygen is mixed with the fuel. There are two types of explosions: **deflagrations** and **detonations**.

Deflagration

Recall that the source of oxygen in a fire is in the air that surrounds the fuel in the form of O_2 and that activation energy is needed to break the oxygen bonds before the fire can take place (see Equation 1).

Equation 1:

$$O_2 \rightarrow 2O$$

This is partly responsible for the slow speed of the combustion in a fire relative to that in an explosion. In a deflagration, the oxygen is physically mixed with the fuel and is in a form where the O is bonded to other atoms that form weaker bonds than in

O_2, and thus require less activation energy to break. An example of an explosive that deflagrates when activated is **black powder**. Black powder is one of the oldest known explosives. It is composed of potassium nitrate (KNO_3), charcoal (carbon) and sulfur in a weight ratio of 15:3:2. The ingredients are all powders and are finely divided and mixed together. The activation energy to begin the combustion is supplied by a match or a spark. When ignited, the reaction will produce gases that escape at velocities of up to the speed of sound (740 miles per hour or about 1,100 feet per second). Explosions that produce escaping gases of velocities less than the speed of sound are referred to as **low explosives**.

Another low explosive that has been used in terrorist attacks, such as the Murrah Federal Building in Oklahoma City in the US, is ANFO. In the Oklahoma City bombing, a rented truck was filled with ANFO, and parked in front of the Murrah building. There is some evidence that the bolts that held the side of the truck nearest the building were loosened so that the explosion would be directed preferentially towards the building. The explosive was detonated remotely. Although ANFO is a low explosive, the power of this bomb was increased because the explosive was confined to the closed space of the truck. Pressure from the hot gases built up in the truck until the sides ruptured. The high pressure served to propel the gases at high velocities in all directions. This is another example of how confinement can magnify the effects of a burning or conflagration.

Detonation

A detonation is essentially an instantaneous explosion. It is so powerful that escaping gases travel at speeds greater than the speed of sound. Such explosives are termed **high explosives**. The tremendous forces produced by high explosives push the surrounding air with such power that they can collapse buildings and move huge amounts of earth. In order for high explosives to react so quickly, the oxygen is chemically incorporated into the fuel. The fuel contains several oxygen atoms as part of its structure. Some high explosives have very low activation energy and can detonate with only a small disturbance. Others are very stable and need another explosive to cause detonation.

Initiating and non-initiating high explosives

There are two types of high explosives: **initiating** and **non-initiating**. These are also called **primary** and **secondary** high explosives. Initiating explosives are relatively sensitive to detonation. The extreme example of this is nitroglycerine, a syrupy liquid that is so sensitive that a small shock such as shaking or dropping it can cause detonation. Non-initiating explosives such as dynamite or TNT require a **booster** charge such as PETN (Pentaerythritol Tetranitrate).

High explosives are often modified for specialized uses. One of the more important of these advances was the development of *plastique* (plastic) explosives. These generally contain PETN and/or other high explosives mixed with a polymer plastic to the consistency of clay, so that they can be shaped or molded to direct their blast in particular ways. They are often used for demolition, especially when a large building must be destroyed with minimum scattering of debris. Just a few pounds of high explosives can bring down a large building: the charges are set in various locations and timed to detonate at particular intervals, so that the building seems to implode. Footage showing the demolition of a Las Vegas casino with just 195 pounds of explosive is available on YouTube.

Improvised explosive devices

The news is full of stories of bomb explosions in war-torn areas of the world. Some of these are very powerful and cause great damage. Others are more portable and are often strapped to someone's body; the bomber detonates the device, killing themselves and others in the immediate area. Although a few of these terrorist bombs are very sophisticated, the vast majority are simple, "homemade" devices, collectively called **Improvised Explosive Devices (IEDs)**. Most IEDs are made from low explosives, such as smokeless powder, but some are made with high explosives. A typical IED is a pipe bomb, made from a length of metal or plastic pipe filled with an explosive, capped at both ends, and a wire inserted through one end. Anything that can create a spark, such as a battery, can be used to detonate the bomb.

Anatomy of an explosion

When a bomb explodes there are two phases of damage. The first is called the **positive pressure phase**. The bomb produces high heat and pressure. Hot gases and surrounding air are quickly heated and their pressure increases rapidly. The air and gas products as well as bomb fragments escape from the **bomb seat** (point of origin) in all directions. The high-pressure front causes concussive damage to objects in the path of the explosion. Some IEDs are filled with nails or other hard objects that create shrapnel when the device explodes. These small missiles act like tiny bullets when they strike people or objects, and are capable of great damage.

After the hot air and gas products are pushed away from the bomb seat, a partial vacuum is created at the site. This vacuum creates a **negative pressure phase** wherein air rushes back to the bomb seat at high velocity to fill the vacuum. This rush-

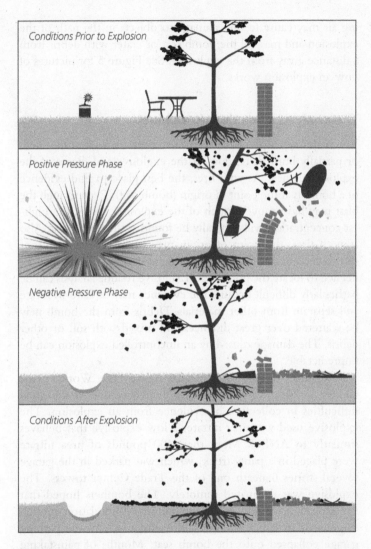

Figure 5 The two phases of an explosion that show how damage can be distributed

ing air may cause further damage to objects in the path of the explosion and may fill the bomb seat or crater with debris from a distance away from the explosion. See Figure 5 for pictures of how an explosion works.

The analysis of explosive residues

The major types of evidence from a bomb scene are unburned, or partially burned, residues of the explosive and pieces of the explosive device. As with fires, the best place to find evidence of a bomb is at the point of origin (bomb seat). Even though the blast may have moved much of the explosion debris, the highest concentration will generally be found at the bomb seat. Also as with fires, the point of origin may be buried beneath tons of rubble, and careful removal of many layers of debris will be needed to locate the bomb seat. Explosive residue analysis can be particularly difficult because the evidence may be hard to locate and separate from other materials. Debris from the bomb may be scattered over great distances and mixed with soil or other debris. The damage caused by an uncontrolled explosion can be unpredictable.

The first attempt (in 1993) to destroy the World Trade Center in New York provides a vivid example of the great difficulties in collection of evidence from an explosion. The explosive used was urea nitrate, a low explosive that behaves similarly to ANFO. More than 400 pounds of urea nitrate were placed in a panel truck, which was parked in the garage several stories beneath one of the Trade Center towers. The explosive was detonated remotely. The bombers hoped that the explosion would weaken the building's foundation enough to cause it to fall. Although it did not, much of the parking garage collapsed onto the bomb seat. Months of painstaking work were needed to remove the debris layer by layer to get to the point of origin, from which parts of the truck and explosive residue were recovered. Investigators were able to determine that the explosive was urea nitrate because they found residues near the bomb seat.

Finding parts of the explosive device can be very important, especially in terrorist bombings. The vast majority of terrorist bombs are homemade devices and terrorist groups tend to use the same technology each time; thus, even small pieces of the device that set off the bomb can yield important clues about who made it or how it was made and detonated. Locating unburned explosive material can also be very important: this material can be directly analyzed by instrumental and other methods and the exact explosive identified. Finding pieces of a device in large amounts of rubble can involve painstaking searching and sifting. In many bombing cases, large quantities of debris, such as soil, must be physically sifted to find particles of the explosive and pieces of the device and detonator. This is tedious work but can pay big dividends to those investigating the incident.

Particles of detonated explosive decompose and may be difficult to recognize or analyze. Many explosives contain oxygen in the form of nitrites (nitrogen dioxide, NO_2) or nitrates (nitrogen trioxide, NO_3); black powder contains potassium nitrate, and smokeless powders contain nitroglycerine (glyceryl trinitrate), as does dynamite. A common test for explosive residues, the **Griess test**, looks for the presence of nitrates in chemical debris. The Griess test must be interpreted very carefully: for example, soil contains many nitrates, some natural, some from fertilizers, some from weed killers, and other materials. These can easily cause false positive results. Unexploded particles of explosive are much easier to identify than exploded residues: the crystals of many solid explosives have characteristic shapes that can make them easy to identify under a microscope. If unexploded particles of explosive are recovered, they can be unequivocally identified.

Recovery and analysis of fragments of the bomb device and especially the detonator can be as important as analysis of the explosive. This is especially true if the device is "professional." Relatively few people can assemble a sophisticated explosive device; like most people, they are creatures of habit and use the same type of device and detonators each time. There are also forensic scientists who are so knowledgeable about explosive devices that they can identify the maker or supplier from very small fragments of the device or detonator.

Fires and explosions arise from the same type of chemical reaction: combustion. Combustion is the reaction of an energy-containing substance (a fuel) with oxygen in the presence of sufficient activation energy (heat) to get the reaction started. Fires result from relatively slow combustion, where the oxygen is contained in the air surrounding the fuel. If the oxygen is part of a chemical compound within the fuel, as in smokeless powder, the mixture is a low explosive and the combustion is a deflagration. Even though these explosions are not as powerful as some others, if confined to a closed space, they can cause significant damage. If the oxygen is chemically incorporated into the fuel molecule, as in nitroglycerine or trinitrotoluene, the combustion reaction is almost instantaneous. This is a detonation and the fuel is a high explosive. Some high explosives, such as nitroglycerine, are very sensitive; others need another explosive to start the reaction. Determination of the cause of a fire depends upon locating its point of origin. Fires can be natural, accidental or deliberate. The latter is classified as arson if the fire is set for criminal purposes. Indicators of arson fires are fire trails and the presence of an accelerant. As with fires, success in determining the identity of an explosive and the explosive device depends upon locating the point of origin, or bomb seat. If intact explosive particles can be recovered, the explosive can be identified.

The next chapter is about so-called trace evidence. Fibers and paints have some similar chemical characteristics, and some common methods of analysis are employed. Both are subject to easy transfer from one surface to another. This transfer can be key evidence in the reconstruction of a crime and the association of a person or object to the crime.

6

Forensic chemistry: Fibers and paint

In 1982, Wayne Williams was convicted by a jury in Atlanta, Georgia, of the murders of Jimmy Payne and Nathaniel Cater, and sentenced to life in prison without the possibility of parole. With his conviction, prosecutors closed the books on twenty-two other killings of young men. This was the Atlanta Child Murderer case, notable for a number of reasons; perhaps the most surprising is that Williams was convicted entirely by circumstantial evidence. There were no witnesses to any of the killings. There were no fingerprints or other evidence of identification. DNA typing hadn't been developed at that time. The major physical evidence against Williams consisted of dog hairs similar to those of his dog, and a variety of fibers that matched carpets in the trunk of his car and his office. These hairs and fibers were found on some of the young men suspected of being killed by the Atlanta Child Murderer.

This was one of the most important convictions in US history to rely entirely on circumstantial evidence. Another unique feature is that forensic scientists and investigators from the FBI tried to determine how common the carpet fibers from Williams' office were. These yellow-green fibers were relatively rare and the fact they matched fibers found on some of the victims meant there was a high likelihood that the office was the source of the crime scene fibers.

On April 22, 1993, Stephen Lawrence was waiting for a bus in southeast London. He was attacked and killed by five youths. Lawrence was black and his attackers were white. They used racial epithets in addressing him before knifing him to death. After the crime, witnesses came forward and an anonymous witness named the five youths. After an investigation, the case was dropped for lack of evidence tying any of the youths to the crime. In June 2006, a cold case review of all of the forensic and other evidence in the case was conducted. New evidence was discovered including a microscopic bloodstain found on the jacket of one of the suspects in the case, and hairs and fibers found on the clothes of two of the suspects. The hairs were a close match to those from the victim's head and the fibers were of the same types as the clothing worn by the victim when he was killed.

On September 8, 2010, Gary Dobson and David Norris, two of the original five people identified as having committed the murder, were arrested. They were convicted in 2012 of the murder. The pivotal evidence was the bloodstain and fibers collected from the scene.

Fibers: the ideal trace evidence

Trace evidence is a term of art. It refers to any evidence that is normally examined with a microscope or that occurs in such small quantities that sampling becomes an issue. Trace evidence is characterized by being relatively easily transferred from one object or person to another by contact. The issue of origin of trace evidence is very important, because of this transportability. Numerous studies have been performed on various types of trace evidence, especially fibers, to determine the criteria that govern their transfer and persistence. The circumstances of a case often dictate the importance of determining not only the physical and chemical properties of traces but also their origin. This is especially true with fibers, which are generally both easily shed and easily transferred from surface to surface by direct and indirect contact. The transfer may happen a number of times, depending upon how easily a surface gives up the fibers, so that fiber evidence may be found on a surface far removed from that of its origin. The journey of this evidence can provide valuable clues about how a crime was committed.

Fibers

Fibers are like hairs in some ways; many trace evidence examiners in crime laboratories analyze both. Like hairs, fibers often occur as loose, single strands, often easily shed and transferred to another host, where they may persist for a long time. Also like hairs, fibers are class evidence: single fibers cannot be associated with a particular object. Some fibers are, in fact, hairs. Wool, silk and alpaca, to name a few, are animal hairs that are used to make textiles, as are other types of fibers. Naturally occurring animal fibers are treated just like hairs for forensic analytical purposes.

Textile fibers

Textile fibers are very common. They are used in the manufacture of clothing, automobile seats and carpets, home furnishings, and a host of other materials. Most present-day textile fibers are synthetic. Depending upon the characteristics of the fabric, fibers may be easily shed. When people come into contact with other people or with objects, fibers may be deposited on the object or exchanged between the people. Once transferred, fibers may remain on the recipient for from a short time to many hours. Fibers can be very important evidence because they can easily be transferred, they may be transferred many times (thus helping to determine how a series of events occurred), and they are often produced for a specific use. For example, carpets are made from fibers with particular properties that best suit this use; so finding a particular type of fiber can lead to a specific source. Fibers come in a huge variety of colors and millions of hues, produced by thousands of dyes and pigments. This means that it is rare to find a pair of random fibers that have the same microscopic and color properties.

One of the key examinations in the comparison of fibers is their **morphology**. If a fiber from a crime scene arises from a particular fabric, then the structures of the known and unknown fibers must be the same. The most important characteristics of fiber morphology are:

- Type: This is the most important characteristic. The examiner must be able to classify the fiber using a standard system. A number of tests help determine fiber type.
- Size: Fibers are generally a few micrometers in diameter. Naturally occurring fibers are measured in micrometers; synthetic fibers are usually measured in "denier" – their mass in grams per 9,000 meters. More dense fibers have higher deniers.
- Cross-section: Not all fibers are round; for example, many carpet fibers are trilobal (three-sided) or bilobal. Synthetic fibers can be one of hundreds of cross-sectional shapes. The cross-section may give a clue to the end use of the fiber.
- Color: Many natural fibers are white or a shade of brown. They are usually bleached before they are dyed. Fibers are colored either by dyeing them or printing a pattern directly onto the fabric. An individual fiber that has been dyed will usually have a uniform appearance under a microscope, whereas a fiber that has been printed may be uneven in color.

Analysis of fibers

When single fibers are discovered at a crime scene, they are compared with fibers from a garment of known source in a battery of tests. Even if all the tests yield the same results for both known and unknown fibers, this does not mean that the known garment is the source of the unknown fibers. It only means that the garment *could be* the source. Given the mass production of textiles, literally thousands of garments could be the source of those fibers.

The two basic types of fibers, **natural** and **synthetic**, are analyzed differently. Naturally occurring fibers include animal (hairs) and vegetable (for example, cotton). These are analyzed exclusively by microscopy to determine the structure and morphology of the fibers and identify the type. Once the fiber has been characterized as natural and identified, fiber examiners seldom go beyond morphology. As with natural fibers, the morphology of synthetic fibers can be useful in identification and comparison. Low- and high-power microscopes are used to describe their length, diameter, cross-section, and denier. Synthetic fibers differ significantly in their chemical structure. For example, there are dozens of different types of nylon. A number of analytical tests can identify or characterize the type of polymer present in a synthetic fiber.

The vast majority of textile fibers are dyed as part of the manufacturing process. The exact color is a critical characteristic that can be used to compare known and unknown fibers and fabrics. Although the human eye is an excellent discriminator of color, it is also highly subjective, can be fooled by lighting conditions, and doesn't provide a quantitative result that can be shown in court.

Sometimes it is possible to trace fiber evidence to a single source. Although this cannot be done with individual fibers, it can be done in the case of a **tear match**. This occurs when a

Figure 6 A fiber tear match in a shirt

piece of a fabric is torn away leaving a jagged edge. The torn piece can then sometimes be fitted back to the fabric. This is facilitated if the fabric has a dye pattern in it. Figure 6 shows a tear match in a shirt.

Transfer and persistence of fibers

A young girl, wearing a red, acrylic-fiber dress, is kidnapped and driven away in a kidnapper's car. Later, she is rescued by the police. The accused kidnapper is arrested and his car impounded and searched. Some red fibers are found on the front passenger seat and the floor of the car, which are entirely different from those that make up the fabric of the car's seat and carpeting. The fibers are compared with those from the girl's dress and found to be similar in all tests. Even though these fibers cannot be definitely matched to the dress, they are powerful circumstantial evidence of association. They provide evidence that the girl was probably in that car, although nothing can be determined about when.

The characteristics of ease of transfer and persistence of materials such as fibers makes them more powerful as evidence than would otherwise be the case, because the ease with which they are transferred from place to place yields information about the locations of the garment or textile before, during, and after the crime. The transfer of trace evidence such as fibers can occur in a number of ways: they can fall off a garment and land on another surface; be rubbed off by incidental contact with another object or person; or be forcibly removed by prolonged or violent contact with another person or object. These are the most common types of transfer.

Direct transfer of fibers from a source to another surface is termed **primary transfer**. On average, about half of the fibers in a primary transfer are transferred off the surface within four hours. If the fibers are transferred to another surface by contact, this is called a **secondary transfer**. The fibers may be transferred again in a **tertiary transfer**, and so on. An example will explain this: if a person wearing a red sweater made of acrylic fibers sits on a car seat, some of the fibers will undergo primary transfer to the car seat. When that person gets out of the car, some of the fibers will remain. If another person wearing a black suit then sits in the car, some of the red acrylic fibers from the first person's sweater will be transferred to the black suit. Relative to the original source of the red fibers, this is a secondary transfer. When the person in the black suit gets out of the car and sits on their couch, some of the red acrylic fibers may be transferred again: a tertiary transfer.

Paints and similar coatings

There are, of course, practical limits to detecting fibers that have arisen from multiple transfers. Human and animal hairs are subject to the same transfer processes; more dense materials such as glass, may also be transferred directly from surface to surface but, being heavier, will usually drop to the floor before undergoing additional transfers. This type of evidence includes paints and other coating, such as varnishes, plastics, synthetic rubber, and similar materials. These substances are made up primarily of polymers, many of which are similar to fibers but with cross-linked strands that form a two-dimensional film. By far the most common type of evidence of this type is paint; most of this section will be devoted to paint analysis.

Paint chemistry is among the most complex and difficult types of industrial chemistry; paint chemists spend their entire careers developing an understanding of how paints work. For the purposes of this book, paint is a type of coating used for decorative and/or protective purposes. It consists mainly of two components: **pigments** and **binders** (also called **film formers** or **vehicles**); other components help it dry, extend, thicken or thin it, make it shiny or dull, washable, or long lasting. Pigments and binders are found in almost all paints, whereas the others are present only when needed.

To understand the nature of paint, it is necessary to review the difference between a **solution** and a **suspension**. A solution is a mixture in which one or more components (the **solute**) are dissolved in another (the **solvent**); as long as there is sufficient solvent present, the solute stays dissolved. If you dump some table salt into water and stir it up, the salt dissolves in the water and stays dissolved, unless the water evaporates. Two liquids can also be a solution; commercial antifreeze is a solution of propylene glycol in water and household bleach is a (approximately) 10% solution of sodium hypochlorite in water. Some gases dissolve in water; carbon dioxide dissolved in water makes carbonated water. There are even gas solutions – all gases dissolve each other in all proportions.

In a suspension, a solid is added to a liquid but doesn't dissolve. In many cases, the solid is very finely divided and will suspend itself throughout the liquid. Suspensions in liquids aren't permanent; eventually, the solid will settle out and sink to the bottom. This happens in milk, where fats and proteins are suspended in the watery part. Blood is both a solution and a suspension: the red and white blood cells are suspended in the plasma, which is a solution. Paints are suspensions in which finely divided particles of pigment are suspended within the binder. Over time, the pigments and other suspended solids settle to the bottom: open an old can of paint and you notice that a watery, perhaps colorless, liquid is at the top, while the pigment has settled to the bottom. If you vigorously stir the paint, the pigment becomes suspended within the binder again. When the paint is applied to a surface, the polymers within the binder form a hardened film. The suspended pigment particles will be suspended permanently (at least as long as the film lasts), coating and coloring the surface.

Other coatings, such as wood stains, contain dissolved dyes rather than suspended pigments. When the solvent evaporates, the dyes are left behind to color the surface. There is no polymer to harden; the stain merely colors the surface. Varnishes contain a binder but usually no pigments or dyes. The purpose of a varnish is to coat and protect a surface, but not color it.

Types of paint

For forensic purposes, paints are categorized by their use. There are three basic types:

- **Automotive paints**: by far the most important and commonly encountered paints in forensic science. (Automobiles are widely used in crimes, and many accidents involve cars and trucks.) Automobiles are always painted with several layers of paint, each of a different type. The layered structure of automotive paints presents some interesting analytical challenges and evidentiary opportunities not usually found with other types of paint.
- **Structural paints**: used to paint buildings such as houses, as well as objects such as mailboxes. They are used for protection and to impart color. The first house paints were oil-based, very slow-drying paints that usually used linseed oil as the film former. The solvents were often toxic, organic, compounds. People could not safely be inside a house right after it was painted. Today, homes are painted with latex-based paints that have water as the solvent. House paints are sometimes found as evidence in burglaries and thefts.
- **Artistic paints**: the oldest types of paints, designed to last for many years. Most are made from naturally occurring oils and pigments. Artistic paints may be analyzed in cases of art forgery, where the nature of the paint and its age may be important clues.

In addition, special-purpose paints are used for protection, coloring, or other purposes. For example, there are special paints that are used to color and seal concrete floors; fluorescent paints are used on some road and warning signs; and skid-resistant paints are used in public places where there are lots of pedestrians.

Composition of paint: pigments and binders

Pigments are generally inorganic materials (they do not have carbon as part of their molecule); many are minerals, or derived from minerals. They are very pure, finely divided, and highly colored. Inorganic pigments are not soluble in organic binders but are suspended in the binder and delivered to the surface by it.

Binders can be one of several types. Some of the oldest paints use natural vegetable oils as binders. Linseed oil (derived from seeds of the flax plant) has been used for hundreds of years, and is still used as a binder in artistic paints. Linseed oil dries by oxidation very slowly; it may take years to dry when used in artistic paintings. When dry, it forms a very hard and stable polymeric coating that can last for hundreds of years if properly protected, which is why it is used in artistic paints. At one time, vegetable oil paints were used to paint houses, especially the outside. These paints take a long time to dry and cleaning spills and brushes requires the use of turpentine or similar materials. Before latex paints were developed, other **drying oil** and similar paints were used; in these, the binder was dissolved in a solvent. When the paint was applied to the surface, the solvent evaporated and the binder formed a polymer that bound the pigments. They had similar problems to the vegetable oil paints, as well as the additional one of having a noxious, and potentially toxic, solvent evaporating in the home.

Today, latex paints are almost exclusively used as house paints both inside and out. The latex binders and the pigments are suspended in water. After the water evaporates, the latex binder forms a film that traps the pigments. Since the solvent is water, cleaning spills, brushes, and rollers is easy and quick. Latex paints can be made quite thick, allowing a lot of paint to be applied with a minimum of brush or roller strokes and making the painting go more quickly. There is very little in the way of noxious fumes. Although latex paints are more convenient, they suffer from decreased durability and covering power relative to oil-based paints.

Automotive paints

Most cars have four coats of paint and some luxury cars have more than one topcoat layer. First, two coats of rust proofing are applied to the car by bathing it in a pool of liquefied zinc and electroplating it. After this, the primer is applied, also by electroplating. The pigments in this paint are designed to minimize corrosion of the body of the car. The color of the pigments is similar to that of the topcoat layers. The next layer is the topcoat, the layer that imparts the color to the car. It may contain metallic or pearlescent pigments that give the paint unique color effects. Traditionally, topcoats were lacquers or more expensive enamel paints that used organic solvents. Today, water-based systems that are kinder to the environment are being developed. Topcoats are usually dried by heat (thermosetting). The final layer of paint is the clearcoat: at one time, only the most expensive cars received clearcoats but today all new cars have this top layer. The clearcoat is acrylic- or urethane-based and has no pigments. It imparts extra durability and ultraviolet light resistance to the paint. Each coat of paint imparts a layer to the overall paint job. A cross-section of the paint on a car will display the layers. Many cars are repainted after an accident, or because the owner wants to spruce up the car, so, depending upon the circumstances, different parts of the car may have a different layer structure. This has implications for how paint evidence is collected from cars suspected of being involved in crashes or crimes.

Paint evidence occurs in two types: **chips** (flakes) and **smears**. Paint chips contain most or all of the layers in the paint. During a crash, paint chips may fall from the car and be transferred to a person, another object, or another car. Because the layer structure is intact, paint chips provide the most information in analysis. There are a number of ways of removing chips of paint from a car surface: if the chips are loose, they can be pried off; if not, a sharp scalpel or knife must be used to cut the chips out. The knife must cut all the way down to the surface to which the paint was applied, to make sure all the layers are collected. Paint smears are much more difficult to collect and analyze; they usually consist of just the top layer of paint. When the top layer is a clearcoat, it may be difficult to see the transferred paint. Smears are often transferred when an automobile sideswipes another object. When the other object is a car, it is even more difficult to interpret a smear since paint from both cars may be mixed.

The proper collection of known samples of paint from an automobile is critical to successful analysis. Like most forensic evidence, paint analysis is most valuable when the unknown can be compared with the known. It is important to collect all the layers of paint in the known sample, and where the paint is collected from is just as important. In general, known paint samples should not be collected only from the damaged area of the car, as foreign materials from the object that the car hit, or that hit the car, may have gotten into the paint and its paint may have become intermixed with paint from the car. The best practice is to gather known samples from undamaged areas as near as possible to the damaged area as well as from the actual damage. Taking paint far away from the damaged area can lead to misleading results, as parts of cars may have been repainted or even replaced and the characteristics of the paint in those parts may be very different than those in and around the damaged area.

Analysis of paint

Paint possesses a number of physical and chemical properties that can be exploited in the analysis and comparison of evidentiary materials. Some focus on the pigments, others target the binders, and others are performed on the whole paint sample.

The most important characteristic of paint as evidence is its color layer sequence. Automotive paints, and some structural paints, contain layers. In the case of automotive paints, each layer may have a different composition and color. If an unknown paint sample and a known sample have different color layer sequences, then the known can be eliminated as a source for the unknown. It is well known that the weakest bond in an automotive paint job is the bond between the bottom layer of paint and the bare metal. Even so, paint chips may break off between layers of paint and not all layers may be present. In this case, the known and unknown may still have a common source, even if not all the layers are present.

The exact color of a paint layer can be determined instrumentally and paint chips compared for color using a microscope. It is necessary to be able to see each layer of the paint to do this. The best and easiest way is to make a cross-section of the paint chip, using a **microtome**; each layer can then be examined individually. Paint **peels** can be made by carefully separating the layers using a sharp scalpel, which can be tedious and difficult. Automobile paints may use different binders, depending on the manufacturer (for example, General Motors used to employ only acrylic lacquers), or the cost of the car. Different binders may be soluble in different solvents or not soluble in any common solvent: for example, the acrylic lacquers used in GM cars were the only automobile paints soluble in acetone.

A number of instrumental analyses can be performed on paints. Some tests are done on paint chips as a whole. If cross-sections or peels are prepared, these tests can be performed on individual layers. The results are compared for crime scene paint chips and those taken from a known source. Some tests are designed to gain color information, whereas others are designed to determine the type of binders in the paint. None of these chemical tests, either alone or in combination, is probative enough to individualize paint chips to a particular source. Only a fracture-match examination, in which the paint chip fits into its source like a piece of a jigsaw puzzle, is potentially an individualizing test.

Fibers are classic examples of trace evidence. Most textile fibers in use today are synthetic. In addition to microscopic structure analysis, characteristics such as denier, color, diameter, and length can be used to characterize synthetic fibers. In addition, chemical tests are used to determine the chemical properties of the fibers and can classify them by type. Fibers cannot be individualized to a particular source.

Paints, like fibers, are polymers but the strands are cross-linked so that the polymer forms sheets. Paints are made up of binders that hold the pigments on the surface and pigments that impart color to the paint. Other additives give paint desirable characteristics. Automotive paints are the most commonly found types of paint evidence. Every automobile is painted with several layers of different types of paints, including rustproofing layers, primer, topcoat, and clearcoat. Physical properties of paint, including color layer sequence, are measured. Paint is normally class evidence unless it can be fracture-matched back to a source; a rare occurrence.

The next chapter of this book is about glass and soils. Although they are commonly encountered in urban and rural environments and thus often turn up as evidence at crime scenes, many forensic science laboratories do not pay them much analytical attention. This is especially true of soil, which is mostly treated as a matrix for shoeprints and tire treads and not as evidence in its own right. As we shall see, soil can be powerful evidence in the hands of an experienced forensic chemist or geologist. It is somewhat surprising that glass, so ubiquitous in human environments, isn't treated with more respect as evidence. Perhaps it is because glass is so inert – it doesn't dissolve in much and therefore is difficult to analyze chemically; however, it can be powerful evidence in the right hands.

7

Forensic chemistry: glass and soils

The body of eight-year-old Gupta Rajesh was found on a road near Scarborough, Ontario, Canada. His clothing had a smear of oily material on his back that appeared to have arisen from the undercarriage of a motor vehicle, which suggested a hit and run. When police investigated the case, they focused on a suspect who was alleged to have hit the boy with a Honda vehicle. They collected samples of an oily material on the concrete floor of a garage where the suspect parked her car. The oily material from the garage and the smear from the victim's clothing were sent to the Centre of Forensic Sciences in Toronto. It was determined that the oily materials and suspended sand particles were very similar. Sand was isolated from both the known and unknown oily samples; they were put through a sieve and the subsamples were compared. Corresponding subsample layers had exactly the same colors. In addition, the mineral content of each of the compared sand samples was the same. Along with the sand, particles of three types of glass were also isolated from the oily material; amber, tempered, and light bulb glass. The refractive indices of the glasses were the same for knowns and unknowns. Some of the same glass and soil particles were also found in the suspect's car. The scientist who examined this evidence testified at the suspect's murder trial that there was a high probability that the victim had been in both the garage and the car.

Chapter 6 covered some common types of trace evidence in criminal cases: fibers and paints; and Chapter 10 will cover hairs in detail. This chapter covers two other fairly common materials: glass and soils. Glass is a manufactured product, made from sand and other minerals; soil is a natural substance made up of organic and inorganic particles. Soil most often occurs as evidence not in its own right, but as a medium for other evidence, such as shoeprints, tire marks, or fire and explosive residues. In this chapter, soil will be discussed as evidence in its own right. Additional cases that involve the analysis of soil evidence will be discussed to indicate the value that soil has beyond its ability to record patterns such as shoeprints.

Glass

Glass is a very unusual substance: most of its properties are those of a solid – it is very hard, brittle, and has a high melting point, often in excess of 2000°C. Yet, unlike most solids, it is transparent and doesn't have an ordered crystalline structure; its atoms are arranged in a somewhat disordered array, which makes it more like a liquid. Glass is sometimes described as being a semi-solid, a fluid, or a supercooled liquid.

The major ingredient of glass is purified sand, the chief chemical component of which is silicon dioxide (SiO_2). Commercial glass is impure silicon dioxide: pure silicon dioxide would be undesirably brittle. Glass is doped with small amounts of other materials, such as boron, calcium, sodium, and magnesium, that impart more desirable properties. Because of this ability to easily, cheaply, and quickly change the properties of glass, more than seven hundred types are manufactured commercially.

Common types of glass

- **Float glass**: a type of glass that is used to make windows and other flat glass objects. The ingredients – silica sand, calcium, oxide, soda, and magnesium – are heated to 1500°C and then poured onto a bath of molten tin. The glass is very viscous and the tin is very fluid so the two do not mix. As the glass cools, it forms a very flat surface because the surface of the molten tin bath is very flat. This has implications in the elemental analysis of this type of glass. One can determine which surface of the glass was in contact with the molten tin because there will be more tin atoms in that surface than in the opposite surface.

- **Borosilicate glass**: a type of glass made by doping molten glass with boron during manufacture. The atoms of boron fit in holes in the molecular structure of the glass and alter its properties. This type of glass has a high coefficient of thermal expansion. This means that it will not break easily when its temperature is rapidly increased or decreased. If you take a regular glass object and cool it down and then plunge it into hot water, it will break. Borosilicate glass (Pyrex, a proprietary name) will not break. It is used in cookware and other applications where stability in the presence of rapidly changing temperatures is needed.

- **Tempered glass**: a type of glass used in automobile windows and plate-glass windows in stores. It is specially treated so that it is up to four times stronger than regular glass. When it breaks, it forms small spheres that do not have sharp edges. It is made by taking regular glass and reheating it to about 700°C and then cooling rapidly. It can also be made using a chemical treatment.

- **Tinted glass**: a type of glass that has colorants in it. It is used for decoration or sometimes to reduce glare or heat penetration. The colorants in tinted glass are minerals of various colors. They are melted and mixed with the raw materials of the glass during the manufacturing process.

The evidentiary value of glass

The analysis of glass evidence

Glass is often classified as trace evidence because sometimes only microscopic fragments are recovered from crime scenes, usually on the clothing of a victim. In such cases, the forensic chemist determines some common physical characteristics of the evidence and compares them to those obtained from a known source. In these cases, it is not possible to determine if a specific object was the source of the evidence. In a few cases, there are large enough pieces of glass recovered that can be physically compared at the places where breakage occurred. This physical match has the potential for individualization.

Fracture match

When glass breaks, it usually leaves jagged edges at the breakage point. In addition, microscopic stress marks are formed owing to the forces applied to the glass during the breakage. Both the contours of the broken edge and the stress marks are randomly formed and therefore can be helpful in associating two pieces of glass. Comparing these markings and edges is called a **fracture match** and is considered a potentially individual characteristic. In some cases, there are quite a few pieces of glass and the fracture match is fairly easy. Other fracture matches are not so easy to interpret because they involve just two pieces of glass and the broken edge may be fairly straight. Figure 7 shows a reconstructed Molotov Cocktail glass container. Note how the pieces of the bottle fit together in several fracture matches. Several

Figure 7 A reconstructed "Molotov Cocktail" bottle. The pieces were strewn about a fire scene

fingerprints were also visualized after dusting the large pieces of glass.

Class characteristics of glass

The number of class characteristics of glass is very limited because glass is so inert. This limits the chemical properties that can be easily characterized. A few crime laboratories have access to an **inductively coupled plasma mass spectrometer** (**ICP/ MS**), an instrument capable of digesting glass and performing elemental analysis to determine its chemical composition. These instruments are expensive and require a good deal of skill to operate. As a result, most forensic scientists concentrate on more basic physical characteristics of the glass in making comparisons between glass of known and unknown source. Some of the more common physical properties are as follows:

- Size, shape, dimensions, thickness
- Color
- Density
- Refractive index.

Of these properties, the most discriminating is refractive index.

Refractive index

Everyone learns in school that the speed of light is about 186,000 miles/second or about 3×10^8 meters/second. This is only true when light travels through a vacuum. When light travels through any other transparent medium, it slows down and bends so that it changes direction. The effect that a particular medium has on the speed of light roughly correlates to its density. Just as you cannot walk as fast through water as you can through air because water is denser than air and offers more resistance to your movement, so it is with light passing through water. The magnitude of the decrease in the velocity of light as it passes through a transparent medium is called the **refractive index** (**RI**). The refractive index is expressed as a ratio as shown in Equation 2.

Equation 2:

$$RI = \frac{\text{The velocity of light in a vacuum}}{\text{The velocity of light in the transparent medium of interest}}$$

The term "refractive index" comes from the term **refraction**. Not only does light slow down when it passes from one medium to another, but it also refracts. It actually changes direction or bends.

Refraction has several interesting properties that are exploited in the analysis of glass.

- If two transparent materials, such as a liquid and a solid, have the same refractive index, then light beams that pass through them will be refracted the same amount and have the same effects on human eyes and the objects cannot be distinguished. If the solid is immersed in the liquid, it will essentially disappear.

- If a transparent material is heated, its refractive index will decrease. This is because, as a material is heated, it becomes less dense and more "gas-like." This means that light passing through it will encounter less resistance and will slow down and bend to a lesser degree. This effect is much more dramatic on liquids than solids such as glass, which barely changes its refractive index as it is heated.

- The amount of refraction that light undergoes depends upon its wavelength. The larger the wavelength of light, the less refraction it undergoes.

There are a number of instruments that can measure the refractive index of a tiny fragment of glass. One popular instrument, the Glass Refractive Index Measurement System (GRIM), developed by a company in England, takes advantage of the fact that a piece of glass suspended in a liquid of known refractive index will essentially disappear when the glass has the same refractive index as the liquid.

Density

Another important class characteristic of glass is its density (its mass divided by its volume). For large, regular objects such as marbles or cubes, density is easy to measure. One finds the weight of the object and determines its volume by mathematical formula and then takes the quotient. For large, irregular objects, the volume can be determined by displacement of water or some other liquid in which the object is not soluble. The object is immersed in a known volume of the liquid. The volume will increase by the volume of the object. The volume of the liquid is subtracted from the total volume and the difference is the volume of the object.

With tiny pieces of glass, some no larger than the dot on the letter "i", density has to be measured indirectly since trying to measure it by liquid displacement would be too inaccurate. Sometimes laboratories will use a **density gradient tube**. A tube is filled with two immiscible liquids, one of which is more dense than any glass and the other less dense. The liquids are layered in the tube so that the density is highest at the bottom and decreases smoothly higher up the tube. When a piece of glass is added to the tube, it will sink until it reaches a point in the tube where the liquid and the glass have the same density. Then it will stop sinking and remain suspended. The liquid in the tube can be calibrated for density using a series of glass beads of known densities. Particles of known and unknown glass can be added to the tube at the same time. If they are suspended at the same point in the liquid, they must have the same density. This can be a very accurate and precise test for density of small particles.

Color

Many glass objects are colored for decorative purposes, or to exclude light, which can damage the contents inside, such as wine. Dyes are added to the glass during manufacture, when the glass is molten. It is not usually practical to determine the chemical composition of the dye because the glass is too inert, so the dye color is exactly determined instrumentally. The most one can say about this test is that one piece of glass is the same color as another piece. When a fracture match is not possible, many forensic chemists will determine some combination of refractive index, color, and density in order to provide some evidence of association or eliminate an object as the source for glass evidence. None of these tests alone or in combination can individualize a glass fragment to a single object and there are no reliable population statistics that would permit a conclusion of the probability or likelihood that two pieces of glass have a common source. Because glass is so common in the environment, however, even tentative associations can be important evidence.

Soil

Soil is made up of crushed rocks and minerals mixed with decayed plant and animal material (**humus**). Its composition can range from almost entirely crushed rock (for example, beach sand) to almost all humus (for example, peat). Soil can be difficult to categorize; it takes a good deal of skill to identify its components. For these reasons, most forensic science laboratories do not analyze soil evidence except when a person has left a shoeprint or a car has left a tire mark in the soil. This is unfortunate, because soil can tell us a good deal about where a person or object has been.

Walter Osborne (later identified as Joseph Corbett, Jr.) planned to kidnap Adolph Coors (of the Coors Brewing Company family) from his ranch near Morrison, Colorado, and hold him for ransom. Osborne got a job at the Coors Brewery and so was able to track Coors and learn his habits, especially his comings and goings from the ranch to the brewery. The kidnapping took place in 1960 at a bridge near the Coors ranch. Coors tried to escape; in the ensuing fight, he was shot and killed. Osborne put Coors's body in the trunk of his yellow Mercury and, on unpaved roads, drove first south, then west, then climbed into the Rocky Mountains. At an elevation of approximately 7,200 feet, he dumped the body near a religious compound: it would not be found until almost seven months later. Osborne fled Colorado and headed east to New Jersey, where he hid the car on a barrier island and set it on fire. In the meantime, the FBI had begun an investigation into the disappearance of Adolph Coors. They identified Walter Osborne and were able to trace him to New Jersey.

Osborne had tried to cover his tracks, but he was tripped up by soil analysis. The Coors ranch is near a geological formation known as a "Dakota Hogback." These formations are made up chiefly of Dakota sandstone, underlain by gray, green, and maroon varieties of clay, shale, limestone, and sandstone. The dirt road near the ranch where the botched kidnapping happened was essentially eroded, pulverized pieces of the hogback. As Osborne fled south with Coors's body, he traveled on more unpaved roads, characterized by quantities of pink feldspar and granite dust, lower in iron and magnesium than the rocks of the Coors ranch area. As Osborne turned west and climbed, the roads were made up of the very distinctive "Pike's Peak" granite, and the roads of the barrier island in New Jersey were made of black slag and drifted sand.

When the FBI recovered the burned car, they took samples of soil from its wheel wells and underside. As these deposits built up during Osborne's journey after Coors's murder, they "wrote" his itinerary. Four layers of soil deposits were found, characteristic of soils at places where the car was known to have been: the outer layer contained material similar to the New Jersey island where Osborne burned the car; the next layer contained Pike's Peak granite, of the same type as that of the location where Coors's body was found; the layer below that had pink feldspars characteristic of Rocky Mountain roads; and the innermost layer had materials similar to those found in the Dakota Hogback near the Coors ranch. The soils told the story of where the vehicle had been during its journey. Even though none of these soil samples could definitely be traced to a particular location, together they were irrefutable evidence of the car's journey.

Soil as evidence

Soil evidence presents a number of challenges to forensic scientists, which may be why few laboratories take the time to analyze it. Its complex chemical and physical properties vary considerably from place to place; studies have shown that soil profiles may differ markedly within just a few meters. There is no forensic classification scheme for soils, which means there is, potentially, an infinite number of soil types, making it difficult to reach meaningful conclusions about associations among soil samples. Because of this, there are no soil databases that itemize the probability of finding a particular soil in a particular place. However, soils can be quite locally specific; if two soil samples have the same chemical and physical profile, the likelihood that they came from the same area is quite high.

Soils come in a variety of particle sizes, ranging from fine silt to large lumps of rock. The weight fraction of a particular particle size can be an important characteristic of a soil sample and is an easily determined property. In this analysis, the known and unknown soil samples are dried for the same time at the same temperature. The soil is sieved, using a nested set of sieves, in which each successive sieve has a finer mesh. A carefully weighed sample of a soil is gently shaken so that the particles distribute themselves among the different mesh sieves. The soil fraction in each sieve is then weighed.

Sometimes it is possible to characterize soils by their color. The color of a soil comes from its mineral and moisture content. Many minerals have characteristic colors: for example, copper minerals are green or blue and iron minerals red or brown. Soils can be examined visually, or sometimes the minerals can be dissolved in water: if there are enough colored minerals in the soil, they will tint the water. The color of the dissolved minerals can then be determined instrumentally. If two soil samples have exactly the same color spectrum, it can be concluded that they contain the same types of colored minerals in approximately the same relative concentrations.

These three chapters on forensic chemistry vividly illustrate the pivotal role that trace chemical evidence can play in crime reconstruction. There are many cases where the trace evidence proves to be far more important than DNA or fingerprint evidence and many cases where biological and print evidence is not present. Unfortunately, many crime scene investigators look only for such evidence, ignoring trace evidence or at least emphasizing it less. The value of any evidence is very dependent on its context; a good criminal investigator will be able to work out what the appropriate mix of evidence is for each case.

This is where teamwork and experience come into play; without these, the entire field of forensic science loses its potential to solve crime. This is a lesson that is crucial, but sometimes hard to learn.

The following two chapters explore the role of forensic biology and the fields of pathology, entomology, anthropology, and odontology.

8

Forensic biology: pathology, entomology, anthropology and odontology

In 1935, in Scotland, a large number of human body parts were found in several bundles, wrapped in newspaper. Pathologists at Edinburgh University examined the remains and noted that deliberate attempts had been made to remove identifying features, including fingertips and facial features. Eventually, it was determined that parts of two bodies were present, both female, one approximately twenty years of age and the other about thirty-five. A forensic anthropologist examined maggots on the bodies and determined that the post-mortem interval (time since death) was about two weeks. This was corroborated by some of the newspaper used to wrap the bodies, which was dated fourteen days before their discovery. Police suspected that the bodies might be those of Isabella Ruxton (thirty-four years old) and a nursemaid in her employ, Mary Jane Rogerson (aged twenty). A forensic anthropologist was able to superimpose a photograph of Mrs. Ruxton onto a picture of one of the skulls; further identifying evidence, such as scars, helped to confirm the women's identities. Once the bodies had been conclusively identified, the police arrested Isabella Ruxton's husband. Dr. Ruxton was found guilty and sentenced to death. This crime and its investigation illustrate the power of forensic biology and especially the team approach taken by pathologists, anthropologists, and entomologists in solving crimes.

Many forensic pathologists, anthropologists, and entomologists describe their work as storytelling. They have a body, or the remains of a body, that cannot talk about how or why he or she died. The scientists use the available evidence to tell that person's story. Forensic biology is a catchall term for a large number of forensic science disciplines that include medical and biological disciplines. Two especially important areas, serology and DNA typing, are covered in Chapter 9. Forensic botany is also recognized as a forensic science; although it is not widely practiced, some of its applications include the analysis of pollens, wood, and some plants such as marijuana, psilocybin mushrooms, and peyote cactus.

This chapter covers four related areas of forensic science. They have aspects in common: they are about the human body as a source of evidence; and, with the exception of some parts of forensic **odontology** (forensic dentistry), they are all applied to dead people. Another common thread (again except for forensic odontology) is that an important aspect of their work is to determine the **post-mortem interval** (**PMI**), also known as time since death. Forensic pathologists generally regard this as a crucial piece of information in their determination of the cause and manner of death. Where the PMI is relatively recent, perhaps just hours, they can use evidence such as the core body temperature and the onset of rigor mortis to estimate the time of death. If the body is in an environment where there are insects, a forensic entomologist may be able to estimate the PMI for times varying from days to a few weeks. For longer intervals, where skeletal remains are all that is left, forensic anthropologists may be able to make some estimates.

Another important aspect of forensic biology is to create a profile of, or even identify, the dead person. How this is accomplished depends in part upon the PMI. If a person died recently, the pathologist has evidence such as fingerprints, facial characteristics, perhaps DNA, and other methods of identification to draw upon. The body may be identified by a family member or there may be identifying documents, such as a driver's license, on the body. When decomposition has taken place and there are few or no tissues or body fluids present, other means may be used. If the remains are suspected to be those of a known person, post-mortem bone or dental X-rays may be compared with ones taken before death (ante-mortem). Such X-rays may contain enough unique features to render an absolute identification. In cases where there are few or no clues as to who the person was, forensic anthropologists are adept at developing a biological profile, which may include the person's race, gender, stature, and approximate age. Sometimes there are clues about their socioeconomic status and even about the cause of death.

Having described some of the commonalities of forensic pathology, anthropology, entomology, and odontology, the next task is to describe each of these fields in more detail and show the types of evidence they usually encounter and the standard types of conclusions they reach.

Forensic pathology

Pathology is a medical specialty. Originally, it involved the study of the structural and morphological changes caused in the body as the result of a disease. Today this is called **anatomic pathology**. In modern times, pathology has expanded to include the study of disease by analytical laboratory methods, including the analysis of materials removed from the body, such as blood, saliva, spinal fluid, urine, and so on, for the purpose of determining the presence of drugs and/or poisons and their role in illness or death. This branch of pathology is called **clinical pathology**. The major difference between anatomic and clinical pathology is the purpose for which the examination is being carried out. Most clinical pathology today is done by forensic toxicologists, who work with forensic pathologists to determine cause and manner of death in post-mortem examinations. Both anatomic and clinical pathology are used in the practice of forensic pathology. Forensic pathology is the determination of the cause and manner of death in cases of suspicious or unexplained death.

In many countries, forensic pathology is practiced as part of an investigation system. In England and Wales, the authority responsible for the medico-legal investigation into sudden or unexplained deaths is the Coroner's Office. (In Scotland, it is the office of the Procurator Fiscal.) Coroners are independent judicial officials and can be either medical doctors or lawyers. When a death is reported to a coroner, they must decide if an investigation is necessary. If the death is obviously due to natural causes, no investigation is performed. If not, the coroner requests a forensic pathologist to carry out a post-mortem. If the death is due to anything other than natural causes, a coroner's inquest is held. Inquests are generally public investigations, normally without a jury, that determine how, where, when, and why the person died, and their identity. If a suspect is identified, the inquest is suspended until that person has been tried and a verdict reached. The main categories of manner of death that are returned as the result of an inquest include accident, suicide, natural causes, murder, or undetermined. These are similar to manners of death categories in other countries, including the US.

The forensic autopsy

Autopsy means "to see with one's own eyes," which doesn't seem like an appropriate term to describe the examination of a dead body. Under English common law, the next of kin of the deceased must give their permission for an autopsy to be performed. This has carried over to the United States and is the policy in most states. There are exceptions, when the law states that the medical examiner or coroner must perform an autopsy.

The number of autopsies performed worldwide has declined greatly since World War II. There are several reasons: first, autopsies can be expensive and the cost must be borne by the hospital; and, second, a hospital autopsy is usually only done with the consent of the family, who may have personal or religious reasons for objecting. Autopsies present great learning opportunities for pathologists. Many of the most important advances in medicine have occurred as the result of knowledge gained from autopsies, so it is a shame that these opportunities are decreasing. A forensic (medico-legal) autopsy differs in important ways from a hospital autopsy in that the family and the attending physician have no say in whether it can be performed. In the US, each state has laws that prescribe circumstances under which the body will be delivered to the medical examiner or coroner for autopsy and, in these cases, an autopsy *must* be performed. Typically, such circumstances include sudden or unexpected deaths, those involving violence, and deaths that have taken place under suspicious circumstances.

One of the most important differences between a hospital and a medico-legal autopsy is that the latter not only involves an examination of the body to determine the cause and manner of death, but also requires a search of the body for physical evidence that might yield clues as to the identity of the deceased (if it is not known), or perhaps the identity of the perpetrator in the case of a homicide. Pathologists who are not trained in forensic pathology often overlook or compromise significant physical evidence.

Any type of autopsy proceeds, logically, from the outside in. Often, the pathologist will dictate notes of their findings during the autopsy and these will later be transcribed into written form. Sometimes sketches are made of wounds or injuries but photography is more common. The detailed external examination of the body can be very important. It can yield clues about the cause and manner of death, note identifying features such as tattoos or unusual clothing, and provide trace evidence that might link the deceased with the crime scene and/or perpetrator. The body is photographed in detail, both clothed and unclothed. Wounds and trauma, such as entry and exit gunshot wounds or defensive wounds, are noted.

After the external examination is made and properly documented, standard incisions are made in the torso and internal examinations performed. Body fluid samples, including blood, urine, and other fluids are usually taken and sent to a forensic toxicologist for examination, to determine if there are drugs or poisons in the body that could have caused or contributed to the death. The major organs are removed, weighed, and measured. They will also be examined to determine if there are characteristic wounds or injuries that can give clues as to the cause and manner of death. Wounds or injuries, for example gunshot and knife wounds, are traced into the body. If there are bullets or shotgun pellets still in the body, they will be located and removed. The body may be X-rayed for comparison with ante-mortem X-rays, if the identity of the deceased is at issue.

Patterns of injury and classification of violent deaths

The major purpose of an autopsy is to determine the cause and manner of death, especially in the case of violent death. The most important evidence is the pattern of injury; forensic pathologists are trained to recognize these patterns and relate them to the cause of death. A pathologist who is not forensically trained may not spot the patterns or misinterpret them.

Patterns of injury in violent deaths can be placed in one of four classes: **mechanical**, **thermal**, **electrical**, or **chemical**. Some types of death may fall in two or more classes; for example, asphyxiation (oxygen deprivation in the brain) can be mechanical, chemical, or electrical in nature. The most common mechanical types of violent death are gunshot and stabbing; other types include motor vehicle incidents and falls.

Sharp force injuries are caused by knives and other implements. The type of wound produced by a sharp implement, an incised wound, has relatively clean edges. Forensic pathologists can examine a wound and identify the type of weapon that made it but it is generally not possible to determine its exact size. For example, if a knife has a serrated edge, the serrations show in the margins of the wound, or on the surface of bones. For a sharp implement to cause death, it must damage a major artery, the heart, brain, or spinal cord. A **blunt force** injury causes lacerations, which have rougher edges than incisions. Blunt force injuries can cause death by a variety of means. Firearm injuries are a type of blunt force injury.

Different injury patterns arise from bullet wounds than from shotgun pellet wounds. High-speed bullets from hunting and military rifles cause more damage than do lower-speed bullets from handguns. Gunshots that enter and leave the body are called **perforating wounds**. Some gunshots penetrate the body but do not leave it, the bullets or pellets instead becoming lodged in bone or an organ. For gunshot wounds, pathologists often attempt to determine how far away the victim was from the gun when it was fired. Gunshots can be divided into three types: **contact**, **intermediate**, and **distant**. In a contact shot, the gun is pressed up against the body and discharged. The entry wound from a contact shot will show blackening and swelling. The swelling is due to the injection of the hot, escaping gases from the barrel of the gun under the skin and often causes lacerations. In an intermediate shot, particles of unburned and partially burned propellant (usually smokeless powder) lodge in the skin; an effect called **stippling**. The diameter of the ring of stippling around the wound is proportional to the distance of firing. For most weapons, stippling appears only when the gun is discharged within a few feet of the target. Beyond that, the stippling either doesn't reach the target or falls off when it hits. These are distance shots.

Drugs and alcohol are contributory factors to death far more often than they are its cause. It generally takes a good deal of a drug to constitute a fatal overdose, and many people will pass out before they can take that much. Certain drugs, and alcohol, cause changes in motor coordination and functions that can lead to death if the victim takes part in activities that require them. For example, an intoxicated or drugged driver may lose control of their car and die. Drugs that cause death are most commonly depressants. An overdose of alcohol, for example, can cause the person to lapse into a coma and slow their respiration so much that they stop breathing; the lack of oxygen will lead to their death. In many cases, a person who has taken a large quantity of alcohol over a long period of time will start to vomit, which removes the alcohol from the stomach so no more can be absorbed, but, if the overdose is taken quickly, the vomiting reflex may be depressed and death will ensue.

The amount of a drug or alcohol that can cause death depends in part on the person's history of taking the drug. For most drugs, a tolerance builds up that allows the person to tolerate increased levels. Synergism is also a factor (see Chapter 4). Alcohol and barbiturates are both depressants; although they do not work in exactly the same way, they magnify each other's effects, so that a person can die from taking them in combination, even though a dose of either one by itself wouldn't be lethal. There are no known deaths due to overdoses of marijuana. Cocaine has been reported to cause deaths by overdose but by a different mechanism than depressants. Cocaine is a stimulant; at very high doses, it causes seizures and uncontrolled heartbeat, both of which can cause death.

Carbon monoxide (CO) is a product of the incomplete combustion of hydrocarbon fuels such as natural gas and gasoline. (Complete combustion results in the formation of carbon dioxide, CO_2.) CO is a colorless, odorless, tasteless gas, which, when ingested, attaches to hemoglobin in the blood, forming carboxyhemoglobin. (Hemoglobin is the substance in blood that carries oxygen around the body.) Carbon monoxide preferentially attaches to hemoglobin, reducing the blood's capacity to carry oxygen; victims of CO poisoning die of asphyxiation. Carboxyhemoglobin is bright red; the blood of victims of CO poisoning is characteristically cherry-red in color. Blood levels of CO as low as 20% can kill; levels as high as 90% are common among people trapped in fires.

Electrical deaths can occur in several ways, depending upon the type and magnitude of the electrical current to which the victim is exposed. Alternating current of moderate voltage (less than about 1,000 volts), which may not even cause burning, nonetheless causes the heart to quiver uncontrollably; such ventricular fibrillation can cause death within a few minutes. At higher levels of voltage, the heart stops beating altogether because the electrical current disrupts the nervous impulses that keep the heart in rhythm. Voltages of this magnitude can cause severe burns in seconds and destroy cellular material in the body.

For the human body to function normally, it must maintain a temperature very close to 37°C (99°F). Significant deviations from this temperature, even for a few minutes, cause injury and can lead to death. Although there may be visible burns or frostbite on the body, a person who dies from hyperthermia (extreme heat) or hypothermia (extreme cold) may not show outward signs. The determination of the cause of death is thus often made by noting the environment in which the body was found. Alcohol can be especially dangerous when a person is exposed to low temperatures, as it dilates (expands) the blood vessels, which can increase heat loss; in addition, as a person's intoxication level increases, their sensitivity to heat and cold decreases, so that they may not realize they are in dangerous temperature levels.

The post-mortem interval and the time of death

One of the most important duties of the forensic pathologist is to estimate the PMI. The pathologist's opinion will always be given as a time range, never an exact time, because modern methods of PMI determination do not produce sufficiently accurate data.

The investigation of the PMI begins at the death scene, where the temperature and physical environment is noted. The amount of clothing or other covering of the deceased is also important. The attending pathologist will usually take the core temperature of the body, to develop a preliminary estimate of **algor mortis** (the tendency of a body to cool after death). Preliminary observations of the pooling of the blood at the lowest part of the body (**livor mortis**), caused by gravity, are made and the degree of stiffening of the body (**rigor mortis**) estimated. These factors help the pathologist estimate the PMI if death is thought to have happened less than forty-eight hours before the examination. If the person has been dead for days, weeks, or longer, these factors are no longer useful and other methods must be used, including the degree of decomposition of the body and the activities of insects.

There are well-established guidelines of the time intervals for rigor, livor, and algor mortis, but these must be tempered by considering the temperature and environment in which the deceased died. High or low temperatures and humidity can affect the rates at which these activities take place, as will the degree of protection (clothing, indoors versus outdoors, land or water) of the body. A good rule of thumb for the cooling of a body after death is that, under moderate conditions of temperature, an adult clothed appropriately for that temperature will cool 1°C in each hour after death. It will thus take the better part of a day for a body to cool from its normal temperature of 37°C to a room temperature of 20°C (70°F). The ambient temperature can have a great effect: if the body is found in the desert in the summer, where the temperature can be over 40°C, the body may actually warm up after death! If it is very cold, the body will cool more quickly than 1°C per hour. Numerous diseases cause fever, so the body temperature may have been higher than 37°C at death, affecting PMI determination. Generally speaking, pathologists use algor mortis as a method of estimating PMI only if the death took place within twelve hours of the body being discovered.

When a person dies, their joints and muscles are relaxed. After two to five hours, the muscles begin to contract, causing stiffening of the joints. The process is complete between twelve and twenty-four hours after death. Over the next two or three days, this rigor mortis disappears. These times are subject to the same variations that affect algor mortis: rigor mortis is accelerated by heat and by strenuous physical activity shortly before death.

When a person dies, the blood stops circulating and tends to pool at the lowest part of the body, under the influence of gravity. If, for example, the deceased is lying on their back at death, the blood will pool towards the back and this area of the body will become pinkish to purple, while the upper parts will become pale. The surface that is in contact with the body may leave an impression on the skin as livor proceeds, which may indicate whether a body has been moved since livor mortis began. The livor mortis pattern may be disrupted where the body is resting on a floor or other surface, because the pressure exerted by the body's weight prevents blood pooling in that area. The onset of livor mortis is fairly rapid, appearing as soon as thirty minutes after death. After a few hours, the livor mortis becomes fixed; the blood pressure ruptures the vessels and the blood starts to permeate the surrounding tissues. Once this happens, the area in which livor mortis has taken place changes from reddish to greenish and then to brown. Sometimes livor mortis can be confused with bruises or contusions, especially after several hours.

Some chemical levels may be related to the PMI, including potassium levels in eye fluids and metabolites of various drugs in the brain. The appearance of a film over the eyes is also related to PMI. Cardiac pH (level of acidity or alkalinity), ultrasound tests in muscles, electrical activity of skeletal muscles, and the appearance of wounds have all been evaluated as contributors to the estimate of PMI.

Examination of the stomach contents has been a standard part of an autopsy for many years, because the presence of chemicals or undigested drugs can be important evidence in determining the cause and manner of death. Stomach contents may also be used to help estimate PMI. It takes about two to four hours for the stomach to digest a meal; if there is evidence of food in the stomach at death, the presumption is that the person must have died no more than two to four hours earlier. However, stomach contents can only be corroborative evidence, because there is great variation in the time of digestion depending on the condition of the deceased at the time of their death. Some digestion also takes place after death and during putrefaction.

After one or two days have passed, other activities take place on and in the body that can help in establishing the PMI. For example, the **decomposition** of a corpse begins soon after death and **putrefaction** (where the body becomes discolored and the skin turns greenish near the abdomen and hips) may be evident within two or three days. The action of anaerobic bacteria from outside the body and from within the intestinal tract begins decomposition, which results in the production of copious quantities of gas that cause the body to bloat. If a person has drowned and sunk to the bottom of the water, this gas formation can cause the body to rise and float. The decomposition of the body depends upon the availability of oxygen. If the body is submerged in water or is buried, decomposition is much slower. High temperatures accelerate decomposition. When a body is discovered several days or weeks after death, the action of insects on and in the body can provide valuable information about the PMI.

Forensic entomology

Entomology is the study of insects and related arthropods (crustaceans, spiders, and so on). When this science is used in criminal or civil cases, it is called **forensic entomology**. Forensic entomology is one of the oldest forensic sciences. Its earliest use is chronicled in a book published in China in the thirteenth century BCE, which describes a murder investigation in a rice paddy where the murder weapon was either a hoe or sickle. The investigators determined which implement was the murder weapon by noting the blowflies that were attracted to the traces of blood on it.

Most of the recent publicity surrounding forensic entomology involves its use in criminal cases, but it has very important applications in the civil courts. For example, urban **forensic anthropology** involves the analysis of the presence of arthropods in homes, businesses, gardens, and farms. Cases in which pesticides are used improperly, leading to the deaths of the arthropods, can provide evidence for prosecution of those who misapply them. There are also cases where insects invade food and other consumer products, such as soft drinks, salad dressings, and even candy. These situations often lead to litigation and involve expert analysis by, and the testimony of, entomologists.

The most visible type of forensic entomology is used in the

investigation of death and in discovering the extent of abuse or neglect of infants and elderly people. Although it is most noteworthy for its contribution to estimation of the PMI, forensic entomology can be used to glean many other types of information from the study of arthropods at crime scenes, including the climatic and temperature conditions at death, the location, whether a body was moved shortly after death, how a body was stored, the location of ante-mortem injuries, whether a body has been buried or submerged in water, and sometimes the presence of drugs and poisons in a body. Suspects have also been linked to a scene by the presence of arthropods.

Arguably, the most important contribution of forensic entomology is in the estimation of the PMI in cases where a body is discovered days after death. Forensic entomology is particularly useful when the PMI is relatively long. The basis for estimation of the PMI by forensic entomologists is that insects have predictable developmental stages and habitats, and that they will invade a corpse very soon after death. The presence or absence of insects on a body may provide important clues about when the person died and may also yield information about how, or even if, a crime occurred.

Despite all the applications that exist for forensic entomology in homicide investigations, this science is used surprisingly seldom. Insects are often ignored as evidence and treated as a nuisance by investigators at crime scenes and by pathology personnel at autopsies. Crime scene technicians, who collect evidence, are seldom trained to recognize the significance of the presence of arthropods on a body; they don't realize the importance of such evidence and are not trained in the proper methods of collection of insects. Investigators are told that this evidence is unreliable and that entomologists can give only an estimate of the PMI, not an exact determination, despite the fact that no methods can give an exact PMI. Finally, there are only a few forensically trained entomologists in the world. If untrained entomologists are called in to crime scenes, mistakes are often made and the value of the evidence is diminished or lost, further contributing to the lack of regard for this science.

Insect succession and arthropod life cycles

In forensic entomology, the PMI is estimated by determining which species of arthropods are present on or in the body at a given time, and their stage of life. Depending upon environmental conditions, different arthropods will invade a corpse at different times to lay their eggs or feed off the eggs or larvae of other insects that have already been there. Forensic entomologists must have a thorough knowledge of the life cycles of many arthropods and the time interval after which they will invade a body, which in turn depends upon both the condition of the body and the environmental conditions. A good example is the blowfly. If a corpse is deposited outdoors, blowflies (also called greenbottle or bluebottle flies) will arrive very quickly, sometimes within minutes, and start laying eggs around naturally moist areas of the

Figure 8 Maggots feeding on necrotic tissue

body such as the mouth, eyes and nose, and open wounds. A female blowfly can lay hundreds of eggs in a short time.

Generally, egg-laying takes place in daylight, so, if death occurs at night, laying will be delayed. If the body is indoors, or buried in a shallow grave, the flies will take longer to discover it. Fly larvae go through three developmental stages, called **instars**. During each instar, the maggot dramatically increases in size (see Figure 8). By the time a maggot reaches its third instar, most of the body flesh will have been consumed. Under moderately dry conditions, the first instar of the blowfly forms from the egg about eight hours after laying; the second instar forms around twenty hours later, and the third about twenty hours after that. After about five days, the larva stops feeding and rests. After a few more days, the larva becomes a pupa. The adult fly emerges about three weeks after the eggs are laid. Figure 9 shows pupae of a number of species of fly.

Decomposition of a body after death

When a person dies, decomposition of the tissues and organs begins almost immediately, although outward evidence may not be seen for hours, depending upon the temperature and moisture conditions. Much of this decomposition is carried out by

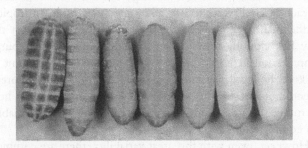

Figure 9 Pupa stage of fly larvae

bacteria inside and outside the body, but arthropods can speed up this process remarkably. Forensic anthropologists recognize four roles that arthropods play in the decomposition of a body:

- **Necrophages**: insects that feed on the tissue of the corpse. Many are flies. Entomologists study the life cycles of these insects on the body to help determine the PMI.
- **Omnivores**: arthropods, mainly wasps and beetles, that feed not only on the body but also on other insects attracted to the corpse. It is interesting to note that, if omnivores are present in large quantities, they may deplete the population of necrophages and thus slow decomposition.
- **Predators and parasites**: arthropods, including some flies and mites, which parasitize on other insects. Some may start out as necrophages and end up becoming predators of other insects at a later stage.
- **Incidentals**: arthropods, including some spiders, centipedes, mites, and others, that use the corpse as a habitat, at least for a time.

There is great variability in the time it takes for a body to decompose. The major determinant is temperature: warm temperatures will accelerate decomposition and cold weather slow it – a level of decomposition that might take eighteen to twenty-four hours to reach in cool weather may take only a few hours in tropical weather. Another factor is the amount of protection that the body has; clothing slows down decomposition, as does burial or immersion in water. Still another variable is the amount of moisture: bodies decay more slowly in dry conditions. A forensic entomologist who uses the life cycles of arthropods to help determine the post-mortem interval must take these variables into consideration.

However, even with this great variability, there are common patterns to the decomposition process. The several distinct stages of decomposition always occur in the same order, although the environment the body is in will determine the duration of each stage, and the local arthropod population will have some effect. Forensic anthropologists generally identify five stages of decomposition. The first three comprise one phase, in which arthropods feed on the body and greatly increase their biomass. Maggots are the major arthropods of this phase, which lasts about ten days in moderate environmental conditions. The three stages in this phase are listed below, together with their average durations and some of the insects that are commonly found on the carcass during each stage:

- **Fresh** (1–2 days): adult blowflies, flesh flies, yellowjackets
- **Bloated** (2–6 days): blowflies and other flies, some beetles, yellowjackets
- **Decay** (5–11 days): some flies and beetles, cockroaches.

When this phase is complete, the decomposition fluids have mostly seeped away and the maggots have left the body, leading to a drastic decrease in biomass. The second phase of decomposition has two stages and takes two weeks or more. The stages are:

- **Post-decay** (10–24 days): some beetles, fruitflies, gnats, some flies
- **Dry stage** (24+ days): some beetles, ants and flies.

Entomological investigation and evidence collection

Some crime scene units have technicians specially trained in the recognition, collection, and preservation of insect evidence from a corpse but the majority of this type of investigation is carried out by forensic anthropologists, who have the training and knowledge to properly collect evidence, make ecological observations, and interpret the data. At a death scene, the function of the forensic entomologist is to catalog and collect arthropod evidence from the body and surrounding area. Insects may be coming and going from the body at any time, so it is important to collect specimens from around the body as well as on and under it. The entomologist must make careful observations about the temperature and condition of the body at the time of recovery and determine, to the extent that this is possible, the ecological conditions since the corpse was discovered.

One important contribution that arthropods can make to the determination of cause of death is that they can pinpoint the site of trauma. Flies will deposit their eggs in openings in the body, especially those where blood is present, such as in a gunshot or knife wound. However, insect activity on a body can also cause artifacts; for example, insects can enlarge or distort a wound. They can also cause what appear to be blood spatters but are actually the transfer of blood by the insects or larvae to another surface.

Another important contribution that arthropods can make in determining the cause of death is in **toxicology**. Even if a body has decomposed to the dry stage, where it is either only skin and bones, or has become skeletonized, with only bones remaining, it is still possible to determine if the victim died as a result of a drug overdose or poisoning. Some drugs and poisons collect in the hair; if there is enough hair remaining, it can be tested for drugs. If there is insufficient hair present, arthropods may have ingested some of the drug or poison, which can be extracted from the body of the insect and identified by **mass spectrometry**. Dr. Richard Merritt, retired Chair of the Department of Entomology at Michigan State University and Certified Forensic Entomologist, tells of a case where unusual maggots were recovered from a corpse. The maggots were very large, which caused the entomologist to estimate the PMI as much longer than was actually the case. The entomologist had assumed that the maggots were large because they had been feeding for a long time but, in fact, the victim had died of a cocaine overdose and the maggots ingested some of the cocaine. The stimulant effects of the cocaine sped up the metabolism of the maggots, causing them to feed ravenously and grow abnormally large. This illustrates not only the ability of arthropods to ingest drugs and poisons from a corpse, but also why it may be important to know whether they have done so.

Forensic anthropology

Anthropology is the study of humans, including their culture and biology. The latter is usually called **physical anthropology**, although the term **bioanthropology** is more accurate. Forensic anthropology is a specialty within physical anthropology, involving the application of **osteology** (the study of bones) and **skeletal identification** to matters involving the law and the public. Forensic anthropologists work with skeletal remains to try to determine the identity of the deceased. They also often work with **forensic pathologists** and **forensic odontologists** to determine the cause and manner of death and the PMI. The underlying principle of skeletal identification is that every human being's skeleton is unique in some ways. Most bones have unique characteristics, arising from genetics, growth, use, or injury or trauma. A forensic anthropologist identifies these characteristics in skeletal remains and compares them to ante-mortem evidence. If enough of these unique characteristics exist in an unknown skeleton and a potentially identified person, identification can be made and possibly the cause and manner of death determined.

Forensic anthropologists not only identify skeletal remains but they are also the principal investigators who collect remains once they are discovered. This process is akin to an archeological dig when artifacts (often skeletal remains) are discovered. The proper collection of skeletal remains is crucial to a successful identification and must always be done under the watchful eye of an experienced forensic anthropologist. In recent years, the role of the forensic anthropologist has extended beyond the identification of skeletal remains; in mass disasters, such as the destruction of the World Trade Center, or plane crashes, forensic anthropologists are routinely called in to help recover bodies.

Some forensic anthropologists are experts in reconstructing facial features from a skull, in the hope that someone will then be able to identify the person. In other cases, forensic anthropologists can superimpose a face on a skull, using a computer and digital camera, to determine if a skull belonged to a particular person. Forensic anthropologists help with facial and body recognition of people in crowds and even analyze such characteristics as gait (the visual characteristics of a person's mode of walking or running) to help identify someone.

The human skeleton

The focus of the work of forensic anthropologists is on the human skeleton. The skeleton is considered an organ of the human body and the bones that make it up are living, functioning entities that grow and change over time, altering and repairing themselves as needed. Bones provide support for organs and tissues, and protect delicate soft tissue; for example, the rib cage protects the heart and lungs. Bone is a complex material, with several layers. The outermost layer, called compact bone, is hard and smooth. The long bones have an internal layer, called trabecular bone, which is light and spongy and adds strength to bone without adding much weight. The medullary cavity in the center of the long bones contains bone marrow, which is responsible, among other things, for the production of red blood cells.

In many forensic anthropology cases, there are only fragments of bone available and the macrostructure described above may not be present in sufficient quantity or quality to identify the bone. It may be necessary to identify the material as bone using its microstructure.

Identification of skeletal remains

The ultimate goal of the identification of skeletal remains is to determine to whom the bones belonged. To enable exact identification, there must be some individual features of the bones, such as ante-mortem injury or trauma to the bone, facial reconstruction, or photographic superimposition. Unusual shapes or features in bone can also be individual. Absolute identification is often not possible; in such cases, the forensic anthropologist will resort to class or general feature identification to determine age, gender, race, stature, cause of death, and other factors. In doing this, the forensic anthropologist will develop a biological profile of the remains. Before the biological profile and individual characteristics are determined, three questions must be answered about submitted specimens: Is the material bone? If so, is it human? Does the age of the bone make it useful for forensic purposes?

Where there are whole bones, or large pieces of bone, identification is usually straightforward. Depending upon the size and condition of the bone, the species may be determined macroscopically by comparing its features to those of various animal species. This sometimes presents a challenge, because some pig and sheep bone and some bear paws can appear very similar to human bone. Sometimes there will be tissue and/or hairs clinging to the bone and these can be analyzed to determine their species.

Where there are only fragments of bone, or it has been burned, bleached, or otherwise damaged, microscopic analysis is called for. In these cases, the presence of **Haversian canals** (characteristic channels that surround blood vessels and nerve cells, found in the compact bone) is proof that the material is bone. The exact species may not be determined but the possibility that it is human bone can be ruled out. **Plexiform bone** is a type of bone not found in humans, but present in many animals. In plexiform bone, the Haversian canals are arranged in geometric patterns and packed tightly together with little or no bone between them. In human bone, the Haversian canals are evenly spaced and there is bone between them. Even with these markers, it is not always possible to determine definitely whether tiny fragments of bone are human.

There is no reliable method for dating skeletal remains but other clues as to the age of skeletal remains may make an estimate possible. There are practical considerations about the age of bone: if skeletal remains can be reliably shown to be more than about fifty years old, their forensic value is questionable. Suppose someone was murdered and their body buried, and then discovered fifty years later. The chances are that the murderer is also dead, or at least so elderly that prosecution would be useless. This means that, where there is reliable knowledge about the age of bone remains, this must be taken into account when deciding if it is forensically significant.

Once it has been determined that bone is human, and of fairly recent origin, the process of identification begins. First, class characteristics will be determined, as part of a biological profile. Then, if possible, potentially individual characteristics that could lead to absolute identification will be determined. The class characteristics will enable the anthropologist to put the skeletal remains in a subgroup, such as "male" or "member of a particular race." Other factors such as stature, socioeconomic status, and time since death may also be determined. Because there is variation in skeletal characteristics among individuals within the same subgroup, it is sometimes necessary to consult databases or collections of skeletons that belong to a particular subgroup so that the range of variation within a subgroup can be known.

Although bones change throughout life in response to activity or inactivity, aging, disease, and injury, there are definite intervals during which bones actively grow. Once a person has reached maturity, the bones will not grow any more, except for repairs and reactions to aging. Thus, the mechanisms by which the age at death is estimated are different for people who died while their bones were still growing (sub-adults) compared to those whose bones had stopped growing (adults). One of the most reliable ways of determining the age of a sub-adult is by assessing the formation of teeth and their eruption through the gums. In most cases, temporary teeth are formed and erupt, followed by the permanent teeth, fairly predictably. There are charts that list the timetables for the formation of temporary and permanent teeth for various populations. Males and females have significant differences in the rates at which certain teeth mature, and some of the charts reflect these differences.

In general, human males are larger than females but this is more obvious in life than in skeletal remains. In some cases, there is little difference in size between male and female skeletons and the examination to determine sex focuses on certain regions of the skeleton. These differences are not unequivocal until after puberty; it can be tricky to determine the sex of a skeleton that is younger than about eighteen. Most commonly, the skull and the pelvis are the areas that are diagnostic of sex. The pelvis has different functions in males and females: in females the pelvis must support a fetus during development and delivery, so, while the male pelvis is generally larger than the female, the female pelvis is broader. The most obvious location on the pelvis where sex-related differences can be seen is the sciatic notch. In females, the notch is quite broad, with an angle of about 60°, whereas, in males, the angle is much smaller. This is a very reliable test for determining the sex of skeletal remains. In the absence of pubic bones, certain features of the skull are good indicators of sex; a number of skull bones differ in males and females, including the brow ridges, mastoid processes, and other areas.

The determination of a person's race or ancestry can be difficult. The skeleton does not contain many obvious characteristics that define racial characteristics. Certainly today, there are no pure ethnic or racial groups, and there may never have been any. There are also different popular perceptions of what a given person's race is and variance in how people self-define their race. A typical scheme for defining ancestry is used by the United States Department of Commerce in its ten-yearly census. The categories are Caucasian, Black, Asian, Native American, Hispanic, and Other. The most reliable means of determining race in the skeleton center on the skull and can be based on either gross morphological examination or by mathematical analysis of various morphological features. A number of skull characteristics are racially distinct; for example, eye orbits can be round, triangular, or rectangular. Other variations occur in the nasal apertures, the palate, and the mouth region. The femur (long bone of the leg) also exhibits racial characteristics, specifically in its curvature, which varies from straight in black people to more curved in Native Americans, with whites in between.

Attempts at stature determination have been made since the beginning of the twentieth century. Today, the most practical method uses measurements of the long bones, or sometimes a large fragment of a long bone. The long bones are the humerus, radius, and ulna of the arm and the femur, tibia, and fibula of the leg. There is a linear relationship between the length of these bones and the overall stature of the individual. When estimating stature, the more long-bone measurements are available, the better.

These elements of the biological profile are all class characteristics of bone but it could obviously be useful to be able to assign bones or a skull to a particular individual. For bones, this can only be done, if at all, by comparing unique features of the bone with one from a known source. Most people receive some injuries to their bones during life. If a bone is broken, it will show signs of the break as it heals. These signs will usually remain throughout life and show up in X-rays. A post-mortem X-ray can be compared with an ante-mortem X-ray and this can provide positive evidence of the identity of the person. Even if a person did not have any bone injuries, there are many instances where a bone exhibits enough variation among individuals that X-rays of these bones can be used for identification.

There are several bones in the skull, and many features, including the frontal sinuses and places where arteries and veins enter and leave the skull, that can be individualized. Where these bones are to be used for identification, comparisons are made between post-mortem and ante-mortem X-rays and also with X-rays of the same bones of other individuals of the same sex and race to ensure that the features are actually unique. If all or most of a skull is recovered, there are at least two ways that identifications can be made. The most reliable method is **photographic superimposition**, which involves comparing the skull with a photograph of its possible owner. One of the newer methods of accomplishing the comparison is to use video cameras to photograph the skull and the person's photograph and superimpose them. Videography has the advantage of permitting manipulations of the images, including fading and at various sizes and angles. Computers can also be used to superimpose images and analyze them to determine if they came from the same individual. The other method of analysis, **facial reconstruction**, is used when a skull is recovered and there are no clues as to its origin. A three-dimensional reconstruction of the soft tissues of a face can be built up onto the skull. Compilations of tissue thicknesses for various parts of the face have been compiled for various races, and for males and females. (A proper reconstruction requires that the race and sex of the skull be known.) Using the tables, the anthropologist uses pegs and clay to build up the face. Some guesswork is involved in shaping lips, nose, eyebrows, and so on, and prosthetic eyes and wigs are incorporated into the reconstruction. Sometimes a facial reconstruction is prepared and photographed and the picture distributed to the news and broadcast media, in the hope that the family of a missing person might recognize it. Increasingly, these physical reconstruction techniques are now being replaced by computer programs and visualization software.

Most physical evidence at crime scenes is discovered and collected by crime scene technicians or investigators. However, skeletal remains are seldom discovered this way. Most often, bones are happened upon by hikers, hunters, or other people, in a wooded or remote area, often near a lake or stream. Because such scenes are unbounded and unsecured when discovered, it is important for law enforcement agents to seal and protect them as far as possible. The search for, and collection of, skeletal evidence in outdoor scenes must be left to professional anthropologists, who are trained in the recognition and collection of such material, both from above ground and buried. If the remains retain decomposing flesh, the search may be aided by specially trained dogs, or the remains located by the presence of flies or other arthropods. Where there is evidence that bodies may be buried in shallow graves, military planes can use ground-penetrating radar to help locate the remains.

The collection of bone evidence from an outdoor crime scene is somewhat like an archaeological dig. The entire scene is carefully photographed before any search takes place. The perimeters of the scene are located and marked off and, depending upon its size, the scene may be divided into quadrants to organize the search. Each piece of bone is carefully marked with a flag or other marker and documented. After the surface bones have been collected, buried bones will be discovered by excavation.

Forensic odontology

Theodore Bundy was one of the most prolific and notorious serial killers in US history, suspected of killing more than forty young women in the western part of the US and Florida. He was captured and briefly jailed in Colorado, but escaped and traveled to Florida where he continued his murderous spree. In the space of a few weeks, he attacked at least five women in the Tallahassee area. Among his victims were Lisa Levy and her roommate, Margaret Bowman, murdered on January 15, 1978. Bundy wiped the area clean of fingerprints and took away the murder weapon, a wooden club. Traces of blood, a few smudged fingerprints, and some semen samples were recovered from the crime scene but could not be conclusively matched to Bundy. Officers at the crime scene inspected Levy's body and found two bite marks: one on her breast and a more distinct one on her left buttock. The one on her buttock was photographed at the scene and a ruler included in the photograph, for measuring purposes. By the time Bundy came to trial, the tissue samples containing the bite mark had been lost. After obtaining a warrant to get a bite mark impression from Bundy, Dr. Richard Souviron, a Florida dentist, took detailed photographs of Bundy's dentition. At Bundy's trial, Dr. Souviron showed the jury the photographs of Bundy's teeth and the bite mark from Levy's body. His testimony was bolstered by that of Dr. Lowell Levine, a forensic dentist from New York, affiliated to the New York City Medical Examiner's Office. On the basis of the bite mark testimony, and that of a witness, Bundy was convicted of Lisa Levy's murder and sentenced to die in the electric chair.

Forensic odontology is the part of forensic medicine that deals with the examination of dental evidence including teeth, mouth, and jaws, and with the presentation of expert evidence in a court of law. Forensic odontology includes the identification of human remains in crimes and mass disasters; the estimation of the age of a person, living or dead; the analysis of bite marks found on the victims of an attack and in objects such as foods or other substances, including wood and leather; and the examination of the dentition and face of a person suspected to be the victim of abuse.

Structure and development of teeth

Teeth are unique in the human anatomy. They can leave impressions in a wide variety of materials, from wood to flesh; impressions that can, under certain conditions, be a means of identification. When a person dies and is buried, the teeth are among the longest-surviving structures and may provide a means of identification long after the soft tissues have decayed.

Teeth interact directly with a person's environment, and their condition may reflect elements of that individual's lifestyle and experiences. Dentists describe teeth using a numbered chart. Each time a person visits a dentist, a note is made of the condition and treatment of each tooth, by number. When a skull is recovered from a crime or disaster scene, this chart can be extremely helpful in identifying the dental remains.

Teeth are made up of three parts: the crown, the body, and the root. The outer layer of a tooth is made of enamel, which is the hardest substance produced by the human body. Humans develop two sets of teeth as they grow. The first set is the "baby" teeth, which dentists refer to as the **deciduous teeth**. These are gradually replaced by the **permanent teeth**. Different teeth develop at different rates, and dentists can estimate the age of a person by the stage of development of various teeth. For example, the first deciduous incisor tooth erupts through the gums at about nine months of age and the first permanent tooth is a molar that erupts at about six years old. The third molar or "wisdom" tooth erupts between fifteen and twenty-one years.

Identification of dental remains

Although there is usually sufficient evidence to identify a dead body, sometimes dentition is the only way of achieving a positive identification. Dental record checks can help in cases of burning, drowning, fire or explosion, and decomposition. All mouths and dentition are different, and a trained forensic odontologist may be able to provide enough information for a positive identification. This is normally done by charting the teeth of the deceased and comparing this with dental records of people who may have been involved in the incident. Comparison of post-mortem and ante-mortem dental X-rays can confirm the conclusion. Even if a person has no teeth, X-rays may reveal enough identifying information from the analysis of dentures and the structure of the jaws and skull. There have been a number of cases in recent years where a bite mark impression made on a person's body by an attacker has been compared with a cast of the suspect's teeth. This is presently a controversial area of analysis; not enough research has been done to settle the issue of whether bite mark analysis constitutes individual evidence.

All four of these forensic sciences are concerned with identification of the dead, determination of the PMI, or gaining other valuable information about the circumstances surrounding death. They are interrelated; very often, forensic pathologists, anthropologists, odontologists, and entomologists work together to determine cause and manner of death. This team approach has demonstrated its value time and again in mass disasters such as the destruction of the World Trade Center and terrorist bombings in Europe. In the next chapter, another area of forensic biology is discussed, centering on the analysis of blood and other body fluids and tissues, and the science of DNA typing, which, although only about thirty years old, has revolutionized many aspects of criminal investigation and forensic science.

9

Forensic biology: serology, DNA and blood spatter

In November 1983, Lynda Mann, a fifteen-year-old girl, was raped and murdered in Leicestershire, England. A forensic serologist determined that the semen found on her body from her assailant was found in only 10% of males and came from someone with type A blood. The police were unable to develop any suspects at the time. Three years later, another fifteen-year-old girl, Dawn Ashworth, was raped and strangled near where the earlier murder had taken place. Semen stains found on her body were of the same type as that found on Mann's body. Shortly thereafter, Richard Buckland, a seventeen-year-old youth with learning disabilities, confessed to the Ashworth murder but not the Mann murder. He apparently knew details about the killing that the police had not released to the public.

Meanwhile, a British scientist, Dr. Alec Jeffreys, had been developing a process for profiling biological materials using a form of DNA typing. His methods could be used on virtually any biological material from a human body including those that were old and had dried out. His methods yielded results that could narrow down the source of a biological sample to a very few people. Using his DNA profiling techniques, Dr. Jeffreys' colleagues compared DNA from Buckland's blood to that in the semen samples from the murdered girls. They determined that the DNA in both semen samples was the same and that it was different than Buckland's and he was released.

In 1987, the police conducted the world's first mass screening of DNA. They collected blood and saliva samples from more than 4,000 men aged between 17 and 34 who lived in and around the areas where the girls had been murdered. When no suspect was developed, they widened the search and still came up empty. The case got a major break when a woman told the police that she overheard a conversation in a bar where Ian Kelly boasted that he had been paid by Colin Pitchfork to give a blood sample to the police, posing as Pitchfork. The police arrested Pitchfork and matched his DNA to the semen samples from the murder scenes. He confessed to both murders and was sentenced to life imprisonment. The Pitchfork case heralded a new era in forensic science. This was the first case where someone was exonerated from a crime and another person was convicted, both with the use of DNA typing.

This chapter will cover two areas of forensic biology. The first, **forensic serology**, is concerned with the detection, collection, and analysis of biological materials. Then the modern science of **DNA typing** will be discussed.

As we saw in Chapter 8, four major areas of forensic biology are pathology, anthropology, entomology, and odontology. Its other major area is the examination of biological fluids for the presence of evidentiary materials. These substances can be analyzed to associate them with a suspect or victim of a crime. One particular biological substance, DNA, is often considered a separate area of forensic biology, but DNA is an evidentiary material in biological fluids and could be considered a part of serology. In this chapter, we will use conventional nomenclature and consider DNA separately. Also included in this chapter is blood spatter, the spatial analysis of bloodstains to determine how the patterns they form can be used to determine how the blood got there and what type of spatter it is.

Forensic serology: past and present

Forensic serology has traditionally been used for several purposes, first and foremost to determine if a stain or other material is a body fluid and, if it is, to identify the type of fluid. In addition, certain body fluids, such as blood, contain substances that differ within the human population, making them useful in differentiating among possible suspects or victims. With the exception of cellular DNA, none of these factors is rare enough to be used to individualize a stain to one person.

Almost all body fluid associations of this type have been made using blood, which is the body fluid most often encountered at crime scenes. Blood is a suspension of solid materials in an aqueous solution. The liquid portion of blood, **plasma**, comprises about 55% of the total volume of blood. Substances dissolved in the plasma include proteins, carbohydrates, fats, salts and minerals, and antibodies, plus materials that are responsible for the clotting of blood. The suspended materials in blood make up the other 45% and include red blood cells, white blood cells, and platelets. Red blood cells (**erythrocytes**) are formed in bone marrow and are primarily responsible for the transport of oxygen to cells and carbon dioxide away from them. They have no nucleus (and so no nuclear DNA). White blood cells (**leukocytes**) are normally formed in the lymph nodes and are primarily involved in the body's immune system. Platelets (**thrombocytes**) are instrumental in blood clotting. Through a series of blood vessels, starting with the major arteries and veins and going down to the smallest of capillaries, blood is carried to every cell in the body.

Blood may be found almost anywhere at a crime scene: on the floor, wall, or any object. It may be on clothing worn by the victim or the suspect in the crime. It may be wet or dry, partially degraded, or putrefied. Depending upon the conditions of the scene, there may be a very small amount of blood present, limiting the types of analysis that can be done or, in some cases, *any* analysis. It may occur in large spills, or as patterns, and come from two or more people. Blood is a perishable biological material; failure to collect and preserve it properly may result in spoilage, the inability to analyze it, or lead to the inadmissibility of the analytical results in court.

Scientific and legal requirements mean that a positive identification of blood by scientific methods is necessary. Good laboratory practice requires properly validated protocols for the positive identification of blood. Protocols for the chemical analysis of blood are very similar to those for any type of evidence: careful preliminary physical examination to spot potential evidence; careful recording of the evidence and its exact location; preliminary screening tests that permit a presumption of the presence of certain types of evidence; and sensitive and specific confirmatory tests of the chemical identity of the evidence. For serological evidence, additional tests are performed after it has been confirmed that the evidence is, or contains, blood or another body fluid. These include the determination of the species of animal the blood derives from and analysis of markers in the blood to delimit the number of people from whom the blood could have come.

Most people think that a bloodstain is easy to spot; that nothing else looks like wet or dried blood and so a visual identification is enough. However, there are many substances that can appear to be dried blood, depending upon the age of the stain and the type of surface it is on. The fact that a stain is dark red or black may or may not mean that it is blood. Sometimes these stains are very small or are on dark surfaces that mask their presence, or the blood may have been washed off the surface. Tests exist to help locate bloodstains even under conditions in which they cannot be seen with the naked eye, and these tests also serve as preliminary tests for blood. The two major tests use **luminol** and **fluorescein**, whose luminescence can locate faint or small bloodstains on objects at a crime scene. Luminol is a very sensitive reagent that reacts with the iron in **hemoglobin** (the molecule in red blood cells that carries oxygen to and carbon dioxide from cells). To exhibit its luminescence, the luminol must be activated by an oxidant – usually hydrogen peroxide – in an alkaline solution. The luminol test is often seen on television: a reagent is sprayed on evidence and the area darkened; under black light a bright blue to yellow-green color reveals the presence of blood. The color should appear immediately and last for at least thirty seconds before another application of reagent is needed. Research has shown that luminol does not affect the ability to carry out DNA typing on blood. Luminol and fluorescein are very useful for locating blood on large surfaces but they are not specific: other substances, including certain vegetable extracts, can give false positive results. At times, it may be useful, or necessary, to confirm the presence of blood; the two most popular chemical tests for this are the Teichmann and Takayama tests. Both are **microcrystal** tests in which a crystallizing reagent is added to the suspected blood. The formation of characteristically shaped crystals, created by the reaction of the reagent and hemoglobin, is confirmatory of blood.

After determining that a stain is blood, the next step is to determine if it is human. Even if the blood is not human, it may be important to determine what type of animal it came from. Most of the common tests that determine the species of origin of blood are of the **immunoprecipitation** type, in which a test animal, usually a rabbit, is injected with human blood serum. This serum contains proteins – **antigens** – that define the blood as human. The rabbit's immune system determines that this is foreign (that is, not rabbit) material and produces **antibodies** against it (the function of an antibody is to attack the foreign materials so they cannot harm the host). The rabbit's blood is now an **antiserum** for human antigens and can be used to test for their presence. Some of the rabbit antiserum is added to the sample suspected to be human blood, either in solution in a test tube (the precipitin ring test) or in a gel (the Ouchterlony double diffusion test). If the blood is human, there will be a reaction between the anti-human antibodies in the rabbit antiserum and the human antigens in the blood, seen as a **precipitate** (or **ring**) between the antibody and antigen layer.

Not all human blood is the same. Both red and white blood cells contain substances that are very similar but contain subtle differences in chemical structure that do not affect their function but which serve to differentiate among populations of people. Such materials are said to be **polymorphic** (many forms). It is not known why or how these differences came about but they are useful in deciding if a suspect or victim could be the source of biological evidence or could be eliminated as the source. Blood contains dozens of polymorphic substances; however, at most crime scenes, blood and other body fluids are often dried out by the time they are discovered and collected as evidence. The drying process destroys many polymorphic substances so they cannot be used in analysis. Those that survive the drying process reside on or in red blood cells.

Red blood cells contain various antigens that comprise a number of blood groups. There are many different types of blood groups but only a few have been used to characterize blood forensically. The antigens in a blood group are all formed at a single locus in a single gene and are formed independently of other genes. The most familiar of the blood groups is the **ABO group**. There are four subgroups or types of blood in the ABO system. Each is characterized by the presence of certain antigens on the surface of the red blood cells and by the presence of certain antibodies in the serum. The approximate percentages of the four types in the United Kingdom population are:

- A   42%
- B   10%
- AB   4%
- O   44%

When antibodies and antigens of the same type (for example, anti-A and A) come together, the process of **agglutination** takes place, in which the antigens and antibodies attach together. The antigens are on the red blood cell surfaces and the antibodies come from a foreign serum or other source. To the naked eye, or under a microscope, it appears as if the red blood cells have become stuck together. Human blood can be classified in the ABO system by adding a serum containing antibodies of a known type. For example, if anti-A antibodies are added to a blood sample and agglutination occurs, but it does not occur when anti-B antibodies are added, the blood must be type A.

The ABO blood type is not very discriminating: even the rarest blood type still includes 4% of the human population. During the 1970s and early 1980s, scientists searched for tests that put fewer people into a given classification. Certain polymorphic enzymes located in red blood cells, and found only in human blood, can be used in blood analysis. Databases were built that determined the population frequency of each form of each enzyme. In practice, at least four red-cell enzymes were typed. The chance that a particular person would have a particular set of these enzymes would be quite rare. As we will see later, this has been supplanted by DNA typing, in which the number of DNA polymorphisms is virtually limitless and, at least in theory, can be used to identify one specific person.

Other biological fluids and stains

A number of other biological fluids occur as evidence in crimes. Three of the most important are seminal fluid, vaginal secretions, and saliva. All may be prominent evidence in criminal sexual conduct (CSC), and saliva may be found on or in evidence in many other types of crimes. Because there are usually no witnesses to CSC, these fluids can be very important types of evidence in cases where the perpetrator is a stranger to the victim and in which it may be crucial to be able to associate physical evidence with the suspect. In recent years, of course, biological evidence can be DNA typed.

Confirmation of the type of evidence present may be necessary to establish that CSC has taken place. Seminal fluid (semen) is a gelatinous mixture of cells, sperm, and a variety of organic and inorganic materials, produced in the seminal vesicles, prostate, and Cowper's glands. In a normal human male ejaculation, about five milliliters of semen is produced, containing about 100 million sperm. Seminal fluid contains large concentrations of an enzyme, seminal acid phosphatase (SAP); although there are other forms of acid phosphatase in some body fluids, the presence of SAP is considered presumptive of the presence of seminal fluid. While the SAP test is the only acceptable presumptive test for seminal fluid, other tests are needed to confirm the presence of semen. The only unambiguous test for seminal fluid is the identification of sperm cells. Sperm have a head, which contains the man's DNA, and a flagellated tail that helps them move. In fresh seminal fluid, the sperm are mobile and can be seen moving around. In most CSC cases, the sperm are no longer mobile, and a color reagent is used to identify the sperm in the presence of other cellular material in the fluid stain. A pair of dyes, picroindigocarmine (PIC) and Nuclear Fast Red, collectively called Christmas tree stain, have been developed for the specific purpose of visualizing sperm cells. However, some men have low sperm counts (they are **oligospermic**) or have no sperm (**aspermic**) and so there may be no sperm in a semen stain. In 1978, George Sensabaugh demonstrated that seminal fluid may be identified if the stain reacts positively for the presence of SAP and if prostate-specific antigen (PSA or p30, secreted into semen by the prostate gland) is identified. Although p30 may be found in some other body fluids, only in semen is its concentration above the limit of detection of the test. A special antibody-antigen test kit for PSA was developed in 1999, and is used in crime labs today.

The analysis of vaginal secretions can be important when a foreign object has been inserted into the vagina. The major test for vaginal secretions is the identification of glycogenated epithelial cells. These cells are formed during menstruation; their quantity varies depending on what stage of the menstrual cycle the woman is at, with ovulation producing the highest concentrations of glycogenated cells. The test involves staining the glycogen using periodic acid-Shiff reagent (PAS), which stains the glycogen a bright magenta color. It is not a specific test, since glycogenated epithelial cells may be found in men and other parts of women, although at lower concentrations.

Saliva consists of water, proteins, enzymes, and salts. There are no specific tests for saliva but a generally accepted test is the **alpha-amylase** test. Alpha-amylase is an enzyme that breaks down starches in foods. Although it is found in many other body fluids, its concentration in saliva is many times higher than in any other fluid. The starch-iodide test is commonly used to identify alpha-amylase. Saliva from crime scenes can be found on clothing or other surfaces, on bite marks, in the victim's expectorations (either accidental or deliberate), or on foreign objects that have been in the victim's or suspect's mouth.

CSC cases present interesting circumstances; where and how much evidence is found makes each case unique. In many of these cases, the same types of evidence are often encountered, with much of the most critical evidence in or on the victim and suspect. It is often necessary to collect evidence from the victim while she or he is in a clinic or hospital emergency room, where the evidence will not usually be collected by a trained CSI but by a doctor or nurse (some nurses are specially trained for this). The chain of custody can be problematic in these circumstances; the primary concern of the medical personnel is the patient, and insufficient care may be given to properly packing and securing the evidence. This may lead to violation of the chain of custody rules, which could render such evidence inadmissible in court. Evidence collection kits, commonly called "rape kits," have been designed for medical personnel; these contain specially designed and marked containers and sample collectors that can be properly and securely sealed to prevent tampering. A typical returned kit will contain blood standards, vaginal washes, seminal fluid smear slides, victim's and suspect's underwear, any foreign materials and debris, dried secretions (such as fingernail scrapings or bite marks), the victim's clothing (if it is likely to contain evidence), and hair standards and combings.

DNA

Recall that the polymorphic blood substances discussed earlier in this chapter have several limitations as evidence. Many of them are destroyed during the time that blood dries once it has left the body. Although many of these substances are polymorphic, there are only a few forms of each of them and the number of people that have one form or the other can be pretty high. These substances, alone or in combination, are not suitable for individualizing blood or another body fluid to a particular person. In the early part of the 1980s, a revolution in forensic biology occurred. (See the Colin Pitchfork case described at the beginning of this chapter.) Scientists demonstrated that certain parts of DNA are highly polymorphic and, further, that there are hundreds of locations on the DNA containing chromosomes that exhibit polymorphism. In addition, the polymorphisms at many of these locations are independent of any of the other locations. This allows the combining of the probabilities of the various DNA types in such a way as to virtually individualize any DNA-containing body tissue or fluid. Using DNA has thus enhanced the potential for associating a suspect or victim with the biological evidence from the crime scene. It has also been shown that DNA measurements can be achieved on almost any type of biologic evidence, even on ancient preserved mummies! DNA typing has also been the most rigorously validated and researched group of forensic science techniques. When performed correctly, with the proper safeguards and controls, it provides a level of scientific reliability and uniqueness that sets it apart from the other forensic sciences. It not only occurs in every nucleated cell in the body but is also extremely stable towards a wide variety of environmental insults.

What is DNA?

Deoxyribonucleic Acid (**DNA**) is a large, long-chain molecule that is found in virtually every cell in the body. Two significant exceptions are red blood cells and nerve cells. Red cells are produced in bone marrow and are continuously being replicated so they have no need of DNA for replication. For the most part, human beings are born with all of the nerve cells they will ever have. Nerve cells do not generally have the capacity to regenerate. DNA can be found in two regions of a cell; the nucleus and the mitochondria. The latter will be discussed later. DNA is the substance that is primarily responsible for inherited traits. The male sperm and the female egg each contain one half of the individual's DNA. When sperm and egg are joined, the DNA strands are joined also. The developing fetus contains a full complement of DNA: half from the mother and half from the father. Thus, an individual's personal traits are all a combination of those from their parents.

Nuclear DNA is a unique type of molecule. Its shape is called a **double helix**. Consider a very long ladder. This ladder has two poles connected by many rungs. Each rung consists of two complementary pieces that are joined together. Now take the ladder and twist it many times throughout its length until it resembles a spiral staircase. The DNA molecule has a similar shape. The poles of the DNA molecule (called the backbone) are not significant forensically. They are exactly the same in all people. The rungs are special, however. Each rung is made up of two **bases** or **nucleotides** that are joined together in the middle as well as to the poles, so each rung is made up of a base pair. There are four bases that can make up a rung. They are as follows:

- **Adenine (A)**
- **Thymine (T)**
- **Guanine (G)**
- **Cytosine (C)**

Because of the complex chemical structure of the bases, only certain pairs can join together. The rule is that adenine can bond only to thymine and guanine can bond only to cytosine. No base can join with itself. A strand of DNA has millions of base pairs and the rules can never be violated. Figure 10 shows the double helix structure of DNA.

At first glance, it appears that there is no plan or pattern for the sequence of the base pairs on a strand of DNA. Closer inspection shows that sometimes base pairs repeat themselves a number of times and sometimes there may be a short or long sequence of pairs that repeat. The important idea here is that there is a plan to the arrangement of the bases in DNA. DNA analysts exploit the plan by using differences in DNA among different people to help identify them.

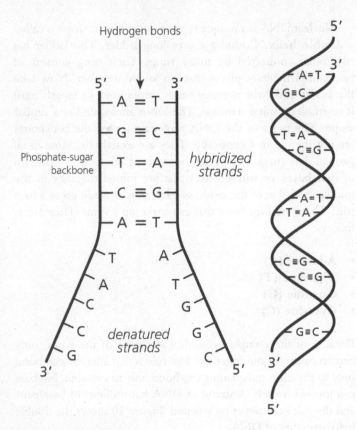

Figure 10 DNA double helix

Why use DNA in forensic science?

There are several advantages to using DNA typing in the analysis of body fluids compared to using the other substances in blood that were discussed above; blood antigens, red-cell antigens, etc. First, DNA is highly polymorphic. There are many locations on the forty-six chromosomes where length and sequence polymorphism occur. Each of these has the potential to divide the human population into segments. Second, human DNA has been shown to be unique to every individual except identical (maternal) twins. More than 99% of all human DNA is identical; it is what makes us human. Forensic DNA typing classifies several highly polymorphic parts, resulting in a high degree of differentiation. DNA typing also does not involve analysis of genes by their function, so that it doesn't reveal anything about a person's traits. Third, DNA is the same throughout the body. You have exactly the same DNA in blood as in hair, saliva, etc. It also never changes throughout life.

Cellular DNA

Most, but not all cells contain a nucleus. Within the nucleus, DNA is arranged in structures called **chromosomes**. In human beings, there are forty-six chromosomes. They are arranged in twenty-three pairs. Each parent supplies one member of each of the twenty-three pairs. It is through the chromosomes that each person inherits their physical, mental, and emotional characteristics from both parents. These characteristics are defined within a **genetic code** that is contained within portions of the chromosomes called **genes**. A gene is a part of a chromosome consisting of a particular sequence of base pairs. These sequences tell the cell what proteins to manufacture that result in expression of characteristics such as eye color, gender, height, etc. The location where a gene (or other base pair sequence of interest) is found on a chromosome is called its **locus**. The human **genome** contains more than 100,000 genes. For example, there are several genes that determine the color of one's hair. Since different people have different hair colors, there must be some variations within the hair color genes that result in the different hair colors in a population. These variations in characteristics are due to differences in the genetic code caused by differences in the order of the base pair sequences. Genes are generally highly polymorphic. The different forms are called **alleles**. Thus, there are alleles for brown hair, red hair, etc. Some hair colors are intermediate between pure colors because a person inherits different alleles from each parent. If an individual inherits the same allele for a particular characteristic from both parents, they are said to be **homozygous** with respect to that gene. If they receive a different allele from each parent, then they are **heterozygous** with respect to that gene. If a person inherits genes from a parent that codes for brown hair and one from the other parent that codes for blond hair, they will usually have brown hair. This is because the allele for brown hair is **dominant** and the allele for blond hair is **recessive**.

There are two types of polymorphism in genes. The first is called **sequence polymorphism**. This occurs when there is a difference in one or more base pairs within a gene. Examine the base pair sequence in the short strand of DNA shown below. Note the difference in the base pair at the position marked by the arrow.

CTCGATTAAGG   CTCGGTTAAGG
　　▲　　　　　　　　　　　　▲
GAGCTAATTCC   GAGCCAATTCC

The other type of polymorphism is called **length polymorphism**. This occurs in strands of DNA where repeating sequences of base pairs are encountered. Examine the DNA strands below.

CATGTAC-CATGTAC
GTACATG-GTACATG

CATGTAC-CATGTAC-CATGTAC-CATGTAC
GTACATG-GTACATG-GTACATG-GTACATG

CATGTAC-CATGTAC-CATGTAC-CATGTAC-CATGTAC-CATGTAC
GTACATG-GTACATG-GTACATG-GTACATG-GTACATG-GTACATG

All three of the strands contain the base pair sequence:

CATGTAC
GTACATG

In the first strand, the sequence repeats twice. In the second strand, the same sequence repeats four times, and in the third strand, six times. Because the repeats occur right next to each other, without any intervening base pairs, they are referred to as **tandem** repeats. Length and sequence polymorphism are very important in distinguishing one person's DNA from another.

Interpreting DNA evidence: population genetics

When forensic scientists compare DNA from biologic evidence at a crime scene with known DNA from a suspect or victim, they compare many sites on several chromosomes to look for similarities. They focus on length or sequence polymorphisms because these are the parts of the DNA that differentiate people. All of the differences in DNA from one person to another represent less than 0.1% of a person's DNA. The reason that many parts of the DNA are compared is because the more parts of the DNA that are the same in two samples, the more certain the scientist can be that they came from the same person. This can be explained by probabilities. Probability measures the likelihood that one event will occur among several possibilities. A common example can be found in flipping coins. There are two possible outcomes from flipping a coin; heads (H) or tails (T). Since they are equally likely to occur, the probability of getting heads or tails is ½ or .5. Suppose a coin is flipped twice. What are the odds that it will come up heads both times? There are four possible outcomes from flipping a coin twice: H-H, H-T,

T-H, and T-T. Thus, the probability that it will come up heads both times is ¼ or .25. This number can be arrived at by using the **product rule**. This rule states that the probability of two or more independent events occurring is the product of the probabilities of each event. Thus, the probability of two coin flips coming up heads is ½ × ½ = ¼. Likewise, the probability of getting heads three times in a row is ⅛ or 0.125. The more times a coin is flipped, the less chance that any particular outcome will occur. It is very important that each event is independent of the others or the rule will not apply.

Forensic scientists use probabilities in a similar way when interpreting the likelihood that a sample of DNA came from a particular person. At each locus where the DNA type (the base pair sequence) is to be analyzed, scientists have determined the **population frequency** of that allele. For example, a particular locus may have fifteen different alleles. They will not occur with equal frequency in a given population. Researchers will determine the population frequency of each allele by typing the DNA of thousands of people. Today, forensic DNA scientists analyze more than fifteen loci and determine the frequency of the allele present at each site. The product rule can be used to determine the overall probability of having all of these alleles. As will be explained later, these probabilities are extremely small.

DNA analysis

Today, the analysis of DNA is vastly improved over the methods used just a few years ago. Whereas, once, a bloodstain the size of a nickel was needed to recover enough DNA to type, today a spot the size of a full stop is more than enough. Almost any body fluid or tissue can be typed and even the material in a single fingerprint or a single head hair can contain enough DNA for typing. DNA typing processes have also become faster, less subject to contamination, and less expensive, and more often lead to useable results. Automation of much of the analysis is becoming common, lessening human intervention and speeding up the process

Six steps are involved in forensic DNA analysis:

- Collection of biological material
- Extraction and purification of the DNA
- Preliminary quantification to determine if there is sufficient DNA to proceed
- Amplification of the DNA using polymerase chain reaction (PCR)
- Separation of the desired DNA by electrophoresis
- Data processing to determine the exact DNA types.

Most of the same considerations hold for the collection of DNA as for other serological material but some are peculiar to DNA. Even though DNA is an amazingly hardy substance and today's methods of analysis are so sensitive that only billionths of grams are needed, degradation can ruin it for examination. Contamination of biological evidence is a real problem when so little DNA is needed for typing. Therefore, considerable precautions must be taken, including wearing protective clothing that minimizes the loss of hair, dandruff, or other biological material from the person collecting the evidence; wearing gloves and changing them every time new evidence is collected; using tools such as tweezers to collect evidence; and making sure that **positive** and **negative controls** are collected as well as **elimination samples**. Elimination samples are known samples of DNA collected from all personnel who could possibly have contributed DNA at the scene. Biological evidence must never be packed in airtight containers, because moisture can build up, which promotes the growth of bacteria that can degrade DNA. Paper bags or other "breathable" containers are used. Wherever possible, if a garment or other material is suspected of containing blood, the whole article should be submitted. If that is not possible, then samples can be sent to the laboratory, accompanied by a sample of the article that doesn't contain any biological material. This is called a **substrate control** and is a type of negative control. Although most cellular material in humans contains DNA, known samples are usually collected by gently scraping the inside of the cheek. These **buccal** samples contain more than enough DNA for typing and are obtained easily and with minimum invasion of the person's body. If blood samples are taken, they should be put in tubes that already contain a preservative such as EDTA (ethylenediamine tetraacetic acid).

DNA is extracted from biological material by breaking open (**lysing**) the cells and then removing and purifying the DNA. This is accomplished at high temperature and using suitable chemicals. The purified DNA is stored for later use in a preservative or in water that is free of any materials that could degrade it. In CSC cases, some of the biological evidence may contain DNA from more than one source, for example a vaginal or cervical swab may contain male sperm cells and female non-sperm cells. Special extraction procedures are used in such cases: the initial extraction is performed using a chemical bath that leaves the sperm intact; the sperm cells are separated by centrifuging, the non-sperm cells are lysed, and the DNA separated and purified. The sperm-cell fraction is treated with a more stringent chemical mixture, which lyses them and liberates the DNA.

Real-time **PCR** (polymerase chain reaction) is used to determine if an extracted biological sample contains DNA and, if so, how much. It is typically used to determine the quantity of DNA present so a decision can be made as to whether DNA typing should proceed. It can also alert the examiner to the possible presence of inhibitor substances that could interfere with the DNA analysis. PCR is a technique that can amplify targeted DNA sequences. In the most popular modern method of DNA typing, the targeted sequences used are length polymorphisms, called **short tandem repeats** (**STR**). These are short sequences, 2–7 base pairs long, that repeat a variable number of times in the human population. Currently, forensic science laboratories are amplifying and typing around 13 to 16 STR at various locations on the 46 chromosomes. The national DNA database (see below) requires that 13 designated loci be typed.

In the PCR process, purified DNA is mixed with a number of substances including individual nucleotides (A, G, T, C) that will make up the new strands of DNA; an enzyme, Taq polymerase, that catalyzes the addition of the nucleotides to the DNA strands; fluorescently labeled primers that attach to the strands of DNA on either end of the STR sequence to provide anchors for the addition of the nucleotides; and other chemicals to maintain ionic strength and pH at constant values. The PCR process takes place in a **thermocycler**, an instrument that can easily, quickly, and accurately raise or lower the temperature of the DNA reaction mixture given above. The process has three steps:

- The DNA is heated to a high enough temperature to **denature** it. DNA consists of two complementary strands linked by base (nucleotide) pairs, A-T or C-G. At high enough temperatures, the double strands come apart between the base pairs, leaving two complementary strands.
- The specially designed primers attach to the separate DNA strands on either side of the STR sequence that is the target of the amplification. This process is called **annealing**.
- Finally, under the direction of the Taq polymerase, individual nucleotides are added, starting at the primer, to each of the STRs on each strand. The result is that there are now two complete, double-stranded segments of DNA that are exact

copies of the original segment. This is called **polymerase extension**.

The DNA is then reheated, denaturing takes place again, and the process repeats. Normally, about thirty cycles of PCR are performed for evidentiary analysis. This results in the formation of 2^{30} strands of DNA. With modern methods of PCR analysis, it is possible to target multiple STR in the same PCR experiment, so that amplification of many loci can be accomplished simultaneously. This means that the amplified DNA will be a mixture of several segments that must be separated in order to be interpreted.

Separation and identification of the amplified DNA

The technique used for the separation of the amplified DNA segments is known as **capillary electrophoresis**. In this technique, the amplified DNA is placed in a very thin capillary tube containing a sieve-like material that separates strands of DNA by size. Smaller strands are able to pass through the matrix more quickly than heavier ones. The capillary tube is electrically charged so that it has a positive end and a negative end. A buffer solution is added to the DNA so that it has a negative charge and will be attracted to the positive end of the capillary tube. As the separated DNA strands pass out of the capillary tube, they are detected by an ultraviolet/visible light detector. The primers that are added to the denatured DNA in the annealing step of the PCR process are fluorescently labeled. Four different fluorescent chemicals (red, yellow, blue, green) are used on the different primers. The various segments are thus divided by the color of the fluorescence of their primers. Each segment is displayed as a peak on a chart and identified by the number of repeats in the STR. Thus, a peak labeled as a "13" contains 13 repeats of the particular STR being measured.

Recall that a person's DNA comes from both parents and each may contribute a different allele for a particular locus. Thus, a locus will often contain two segments. Someone may be a "12, 16" at a particular locus, meaning that a particular STR had 12 repeats from one parent and 16 from the other. In addition to the evidence and known DNA samples, **DNA ladders** are also run. These contain many DNA fragments of known size, used to calibrate the instrument so that the correct number of repeats is determined for each peak. The total alleles from all of the loci analyzed forms a **DNA profile**. If DNA profiles from evidentiary DNA and that of a known source are exactly the same, a conclusion of association can be made.

DNA typing by STR analysis is not a perfect process. Very occasionally, a wrong allele is called by the computer that interprets the electrophoretic peaks. Degraded or insufficient DNA can make it difficult to distinguish a real peak from instrument noise, or mixtures can be difficult to interpret. Research indicates that most problems with DNA analysis arise from improper handling of samples, mixing up of samples, or contamination by an operator. Like all evidence, DNA must be handled with extreme care. Figure 11 shows a 16-loci DNA profile by capillary electrophoresis.

For the above DNA type, the frequency at which it would occur in the Caucasian population is about 1 in 330×10^{21} (sextillion) people. Of course, there aren't nearly that many people on Earth (about 6×10^9) so the chances of finding Caucasians with this DNA profile are almost nil. The United States FBI has the practice of declaring virtual individualization of a DNA type when the frequency exceeds 1,000 times the world population (6×10^{12}). With 13 or more loci, just about every combination of alleles exceeds this value. This is why DNA typing by STRs is so powerful.

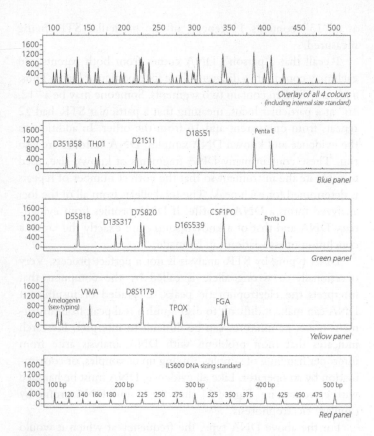

Figure 11 A 16-loci DNA electropherogram

NDNAD: the United Kingdom National DNA Database

One of the most important advances in DNA typing is the development of local and national databases that contain thousands of DNA types of many people who have been involved in crimes. When DNA from an unknown suspect is found at a crime scene, it can be typed and the type sent to the database. There have been many cases where hits have been made even in cases where the perpetrator committed crimes in a different place. In 1995, the first national DNA database in the world was set up by the UK Forensic Science Service. The **NDNAD** contains more than two million DNA profiles, garnered from people charged with criminal offenses (even if they were found innocent), convicted criminals, and profiles from crime scenes. A similar database is maintained by the FBI in the US: **CODIS**, the Combined DNA Index System.

DNA databases have been found to be very useful in identifying crime suspects from evidence found at a crime scene. In addition, they have begun to be used extensively in "cold cases"; cases that occurred before the advent of DNA typing but which can be reinvestigated using DNA evidence preserved from the scene of the crime. Another important, growing use of DNA databases is post-conviction review, in which a convicted felon is able to convince an attorney to have evidence preserved from the crime reanalyzed, using DNA typing that wasn't available at the time of the crime. Several hundred convicted felons have been released from prison, some having served twenty years or more for crimes that DNA typing proved that they could not have committed. Sometimes, when there is a suspect for a crime but the DNA evidence is fragmentary, a database can be searched using a partial DNA type. This may yield several matches and the police can then investigate the "hits" to see if one of them may have been the owner of the DNA. An example of the value of the database in this context occurred in a multiple murder case in Wales. Degraded DNA from the scene was profiled and the NDNAD searched. A partial match came for a relative of a suspect, Joseph Kappen, who had died. On the basis of this match and similarities with the DNA of other relatives, Kappen's body was exhumed and a DNA profile created. This exactly matched the evidence from the scene.

Mitochondrial DNA typing

Sometimes it is not possible to obtain nuclear DNA for analysis, or it may be so degraded that analysis is not possible, as is sometimes the case with skeletal remains. Fortunately, another kind of DNA is found in the **mitochondria**, although it makes up only about 1% of DNA. Mitochondria are structures present in every cell in the body, in the cytoplasm, outside the nucleus. Mitochondria are responsible for energy production in the cell and their DNA helps with this function. There are thousands of mitochondria in each cell and thus thousands of copies of their DNA, whereas there are only a few copies of nuclear DNA in each cell.

Mitochondrial DNA differs from nuclear DNA in important ways. First, it is not arranged in a double helix but is circular. Second, there are 37 genes in human mitochondrial DNA, but the forensically important part consists of about 1,100 base pairs within two regions, HV1 and HV2, that do not have a genetic code function. These regions are highly variable and quite useful for DNA comparisons. Although there is a great deal of variability in mitochondrial DNA among unrelated people, only these two regions exhibit this variability, so mitochondrial DNA typing is not yet able to individualize DNA. Third, mitochondrial DNA is inherited only from the mother, with no contribution whatsoever from the father. This makes mitochondrial DNA typing a useful vehicle for tracing one's parentage back through the maternal line. Every sibling in a family has the same mitochondrial DNA as each other, and as their mother, maternal grandmother, and so on.

Over the years, forensic serology has expanded its role greatly with the developments of blood spatter analysis and DNA typing. These two areas have had a major impact on criminal investigation and forensic analysis, especially in the areas of cold cases and claims of innocence. Blood spatter suffers from the same difficulties as other pattern evidence, which will be covered in Chapter 10, with a serious lack of rigorous scientific research to support the conclusions made by blood spatter analysts about the type and origin of spatters and their role in reconstructing crime scenes. DNA typing has evolved into a major force in criminal and civil investigations. A competent analyst can associate biological evidence to a particular source with a high degree of certainty, if not outright.

Blood spatter

Blood spatter pattern recognition and analysis is a growing field of crime scene technology and forensic science. It has become an important tool in helping the forensic investigator determine what happened in a violent incident where blood has been shed and can be used to provide evidence against a suspect or exonerate an accused person. It can also be a valuable tool in reconstructing the incident. Blood spatter can establish a great deal about a violent criminal incident, including the:

- Type of activity that created the bloodshed
- Point of origin
- Direction of travel
- Distance between target surface and blood source
- Positions during bloodshed
- Movements during or after bloodshed
- Number of hits or blows
- Identification of individuals present at scene
- Establishment of the sequence of events during and after bloodshed.

Blood spatters are a form of pattern evidence. Unlike handwriting, fingerprints, and firearms, blood spatter analysis is relatively new, having first been popularized in the 1980s. There has been little research and there are only a small number of real experts in the field, some of whom offer short courses of one or two weeks to field investigators and forensic scientists. Because of the lack of a research base, blood spatter has recently come under the same scrutiny as other forms of pattern evidence for its possible lack of reliability and validity, and the possibility of observer bias. It is obviously difficult to design realistic research scenarios that prove the reliability of conclusions being made about certain types of blood spatter but it is possible some of these issues can be addressed by aggressive funding and research.

There are many types of bloodstain patterns. They arise from one of two mechanisms: first, blood spatter arising from the impact of an object on the body, such as from blunt force injuries or gunshots. Impact spatter is bloodstains that are the result of a bloody object receiving a blow. The object must have blood on its surface to create this type of pattern. In most cases, the first blow will not produce an impact stain but subsequent blows will result in impact spatter. The exception is stains produced by gunshots; gunshot patterns are often a fine mist of blood. The second mechanism is the projection of blood spatter away from the body, which includes cast-off patterns, drips, arterial spurts, swipes, wipes, and expiration of blood. Cast-off patterns are produced from a bloody object such as a knife, baseball bat, or hand. These stains form a linear pattern, often on the ceiling. Drip patterns result from blood dripping from an object onto the floor or another surface. If blood drips into wet blood, it will form a satellite spatter, characterized by spines that project from the main droplet. Arterial gushing or spurts are easily recognized by an arc pattern, due to the rise and fall of blood pressure, which indicates that a major artery (such as the carotid or femoral) has been breached. Swipe patterns are created by the transfer of blood onto a target by a moving object that is bloodstained. A wipe pattern, on the other hand, occurs when an object moves through a preexisting bloodstain onto another surface. Expiration, the rapid loss of blood from a wound, results in pools of blood and spatters.

The next chapter is about pattern evidence, where the major objective is to associate the evidence with a particular source. As will be seen, this can be a difficult process, whose analytical methodologies do not have the scientific underpinning of drug chemistry.

10

Pattern evidence: fingerprints, firearms, questioned documents and hairs

In March 2004, in Madrid, Spain, there was a series of terrorist attacks on commuter trains. Explosives were set off in the subway system, causing great damage and loss of life. Some detonator caps containing partial fingerprints were recovered from the scene by Spanish police investigators and submitted to the FBI for analysis. The FBI maintains a fingerprint database, **IAFIS** (Integrated Automated Fingerprint Identification System), which contains millions of sets of fingerprints. An IAFIS search compares an unknown print to the database, usually resulting in a short list of potential matches. A fingerprint examiner takes the sets of prints containing the possible matches and manually compares them with the prints from the crime scene.

The latent print from Madrid was determined to be of value for identification purposes and was subsequently linked to an Oregon lawyer, Brandon Mayfield. This latent print identification was confirmed by a second FBI examiner and then by a third, retired, FBI examiner. Soon after, the Madrid police authorities uncovered additional information about the bombing that cast doubt on the FBI match. Another suspect, Ouhnane Daoud, was identified in Spain, who better matched the latent print. This was confirmed by two FBI examiners, who went to Spain for the comparison. Brandon Mayfield was subsequently exonerated; he later sued the FBI and won a monetary award. Figure 12 shows the print evidence that was compared in this case.

How could three trained, experienced FBI examiners all come to the same, wrong conclusion? There were a number of reasons, including the fact that the latent print was of poor quality. However, there was also evidence of what is termed **observer** or **confirmational bias**, in which a neutral examiner becomes biased or contaminated by having information about a case that may lead them to a conclusion that they may not otherwise have reached. See Chapter 11 for a more in-depth discussion of observer bias. Because of these biases, and some court decisions in the United States, certain types of scientific evidence, including fingerprint evidence, have come under increased scrutiny by the courts and the forensic science system. This group

Daoud   Lift from   Mayfield
bomb scene

Figure 12 The fingerprint from the Madrid bombing case that was misidentified as belonging to Brandon Mayfield

of disciplines is collectively called **experience-based forensic sciences** or sometimes just **pattern evidence**. In this chapter, we will discuss some of the more prominent types of pattern evidence, and see how they are used in forensic science and why they are being scrutinized, despite the fact that some have been routinely accepted as evidence in courts all over the world for more than a hundred years.

What is pattern evidence?

Pattern evidence generally includes the following evidence types:

- Hairs
- Fingerprints
- Shoeprints
- Tire treads
- Handwriting
- Firearms and toolmarks.

All of these have common features. The major mode of their forensic analysis is the visual comparison of certain physical features that form reproducible patterns of features or markings. Forensic scientists compare features of crime scene evidence to those of known samples; if there are enough points of similarity and no unexplainable differences, the examiner can conclude that the unknown could have arisen from the same source as the known. In some cases, the conclusion may rise to the level of individuality. In general, no additional, **orthogonal** (based on different principles) tests are used. The forensic examiner must rely on their judgment and experience in reaching conclusions; there is no backup. In some laboratories, these types of examinations are performed by two independent examiners who may or may not be aware of the other's conclusions, but this is by no means universal.

In recent years, following the decision of the US Supreme Court in *Daubert versus Merrell Dow*, the requirement for demonstration of scientific reliability before scientific evidence can be admitted in court has caused judges, lawyers, and forensic scientists to reexamine the underlying scientific principles of many types of evidence, especially pattern evidence. In some cases, previously routinely accepted evidence of individuality or association has been barred from some courts because of the paucity of evidence of its scientific reliability.

In this chapter, we will focus on the most commonly encountered types of pattern evidence: fingerprints, firearms and toolmarks, and handwriting and hairs. The Forensic Science Committee of the National Academy of Sciences in the US paid special attention to the issues of pattern evidence. The Committee heard much testimony concerning the reliability of analysis of pattern evidence and concluded that there was little scientific justification for individualizing pattern evidence to one and only one source and that a great deal of research had to be done to prove or disprove the principle of individualization of pattern evidence types.

Fingerprints

Look at your hands: the inside surfaces of your palms and fingers are not smooth but are marked by a series of ridges and furrows, whose purpose is presumably to provide a better surface for gripping. (There are also ridges on the soles of your feet but these are harder to see and aren't encountered in crime very much.) The ridge structure of your palm and finger surfaces can be quite complex, and it is interesting to question how they arise during fetal development. Identical twins often have demonstrably different fingerprints, which argues against completely genetic control over their development.

The science of the comparison of friction ridge structures such as fingerprints is called **dactyloscopy**. Dactyloscopy employs the science of ridge analysis (**ridgeology**) to analyze and compare fingerprints. Although the use of fingerprints for personal identification has been around for thousands of years, its science is still evolving and scientists are actively researching more objective methods of comparing fingerprints and new ways of visualizing them. Although palm prints occasionally occur as evidence of criminal activity, fingerprints occur much more frequently, and so this discussion will focus on fingerprints; in fact, on prints of the end joint of the fingers, because these have been studied most extensively and prints from them are found most often.

There is anecdotal evidence that the Chinese used fingerprints as a form of signature on legal documents more than three thousand years ago but it is not known if this was for the purpose of identifying the author of the document and there is no surviving evidence that any principles were developed to guide people in identifying or comparing fingerprints. The first organized use of friction ridges for identification occurred in the late 1870s, when William Herschel, a British official in India, required that contracts involving the indigenous people included an imprint of their entire hand, but, again, there is no evidence that he developed any systematic way of linking a handprint to a particular person. The first paper to discuss the use of fingerprints for identification purposes was published by Henry Faulds in *Nature* in 1880. Faulds was a missionary in Japan, working in a hospital, when he discovered there were unique patterns to human fingerprints. He tried to chemically alter his own fingerprints but the original pattern grew back. Faulds demonstrated that fingerprint impressions could be taken by dipping the fingers in ink, and suggested that prints could eventually be collected from crime scenes; he even used fingerprints to help the Tokyo police in a burglary investigation. Faulds was interested in further research and eventually appealed for funds to the famous anthropologist Charles Darwin. Darwin passed on the appeal to his nephew Sir Francis Galton. Galton didn't fund Faulds, but he did take credit for Faulds' discoveries.

In 1883, a French police expert, Alphonse Bertillon, devised the first systematic method of personal identification. His system of **anthropometry** relied on a carefully constructed and detailed description of a person, the *portrait parlé*, which included full-length photographs and precise measurements of the body. Bertillonage, as the complete system was called, was based on the unproven premise that, after the age of about eighteen, the human skeleton stops growing. In addition, it was thought that all skeletons were different, reflected in the uniqueness of the body measurements that Bertillon demanded. Bertillonage was considered a reliable method of personal identification until the beginning of the twentieth century but the Will West affair of 1903 signaled its demise. William West was convicted of a crime and sent to Leavenworth Prison in Kansas. At that time, the prison system routinely collected a *portrait parlé* of its prisoners; when West was being processed at the prison, officials found that there already was a William West there. His body measurements were virtually the same as those of the incoming prisoner and, in fact, the two men looked like twins. Their fingerprints were very different, however. This case showed that Bertillonage could not be relied upon as a means of personal identification and it quickly fell out of favor, to be replaced by fingerprints.

Meanwhile, Sir Francis Galton published a book entitled *Finger Prints*. One of the major contributions of this book was that it proposed that all fingerprint patterns could be put into one of three categories: **loops**, **arches**, and **whorls**. Galton also asserted that all fingerprints were unique and that they didn't change throughout life. See Figure 13.

Once Galton suggested that fingerprints fell into certain patterns, the next step was the development of a classification system. The goal of such a system was to put a set of fingerprints from one person into one of a small number of groups. This

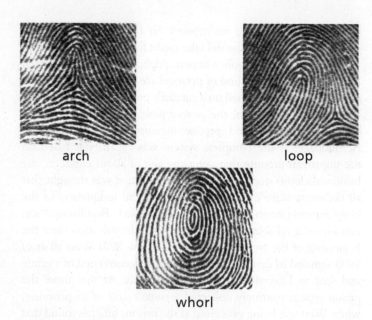

arch

loop

whorl

Figure 13 The three major classes of fingerprints

would make searching through many sets of fingerprints easier. If a person was fingerprinted and the police wanted to know if that person was already in a database, the classification of fingerprint sets would make that feasible. As it turned out, two independent classification systems were developed at about the same time. Juan Vucetich, an Argentinian police officer, became interested in Galton's work and developed the first classification system. It has been continuously refined and is still widely used today in South and Central America. In England, Sir Edward Henry developed a somewhat different classification system. It too has survived and, although it has been modified, is used today in the United States and much of Europe. The original Henry system used five classifications to put a set of ten fingerprints into one of thousands of classes. This worked well until the number of sets of fingerprints in each class became so large that it ceased to be practical as a searching tool. In recent years, the FBI has added additional criteria to increase the number of classes. The classifications developed by Henry used certain characteristics of each fingerprint. These included designating which fingers had loops, arches, and whorls and how many ridges were in a particular pattern.

The origin of fingerprints

The purpose of fingerprints, and also of the friction ridges on the palms and soles of the feet, is to provide a textured surface for gripping objects and holding on to things. Fingerprints arise from the skin, particularly from the dermal papillae, the layer of cells between the epidermis (the outermost skin layer) and the dermis (the inner layer of the skin). Fingerprint ridges begin forming at about the eighth week of gestation and are fully formed by the seventeenth week. From then on, barring artificial means of alteration, fingerprints do not change, except to grow larger as the body grows. As the friction ridges develop, perspiration glands are formed that end in rows of sweat pores on the fingerprint ridges. As perspiration is discharged from the sweat glands, it travels through the pores onto the surface of the ridges. When a finger touches a surface, perspiration residue, sweat, skin cells, proteins, fats, and other materials are deposited. Since these materials are normally invisible, this image is called a **latent** fingerprint. A fingerprint that is readily visible, for example one deposited in paint or blood on a surface, is called a **patent** print, and a fingerprint that is formed in a soft material such as putty is called a **plastic** print.

The anatomy of fingerprints

For the purposes of dactyloscopy, a fingerprint consists of the friction ridge skin of the end joint of each finger, taken from cuticle to cuticle. Although other joints of the fingers, palms, and the soles of the feet may have unique ridge patterns, these have not been studied rigorously.

Fingerprints consist of a set of ridges of various shapes and sizes. The major types are:

- **Bifurcations**: ridges that split into two
- **Ending ridge**: a simple straight ridge
- **Dot** or **island**: tiny round ridges
- **Short ridge**: small, isolated segment of ridge
- **Enclosure** or **anastomosis**: a ridge that forks and forms a complete circle and then becomes a single ridge again
- **Trifurcation**: a ridge that splits into three.

Taken together, the ridge characteristics of a fingerprint are called its **minutiae**. The types and locations of specific minutiae impart the uniqueness that is the basis for comparison of fingerprints. Figure 14 shows a point-by-point comparison between a

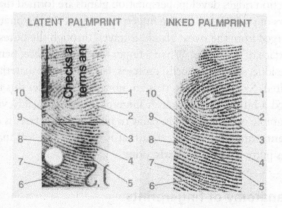

Figure 14 A comparison of a known fingerprint with an inked suspect print

fingerprint lifted from a crime scene and one taken from a set of inked prints of the suspect.

Detection and visualization of fingerprints

Fingerprints can be deposited on a wide variety of surfaces at a crime scene, which is why fingerprint technicians spend so much time searching a scene to recover them. Even criminals who wear gloves at a crime scene may leave fingerprints: gloves may slip off, or be taken off for one reason or another. A glove may even leave an image of its outer surface on an object. Patent and plastic fingerprints are generally easy to discover, as they are left in paint or another medium, or impressed into a material such as putty; the major challenge for the fingerprint technician lies in discovering, and visualizing, latent prints. The science of **visualization** has been changing rapidly in recent years, as new chemical and physical methods are developed and revised.

The method used to visualize a latent fingerprint depends upon the type of surface it lies on. Smooth, non-porous surfaces can easily be dusted with fingerprint powders or cyanoacrylate (Super Glue®) fumes. There are a large number of commercially available fingerprint powders, in a wide variety of colors. A powder whose color contrasts with the color of the surface being dusted will be chosen. The powder is applied with camel's hair or nylon brushes with very soft bristles. For surfaces that have a fine texture, such as some plastics and hides, magnetic powders are often used, applied by magnetic brushes. The brush is moved across the surface of the object without touching it, which allows the powder to cling to the surface of the fingerprint residues without getting into the cracks in the surface.

Developing new chemical methods of visualizing fingerprints is one of the most active areas of fingerprint research. The oldest chemical method is iodine fuming. Iodine is a solid at room temperature. When heated, it sublimes; it becomes a vapor without first becoming a liquid. When iodine fumes are exposed to fingerprint residues, they react to form a reddish image of the fingerprint. This image is temporary and the visualized prints must be photographed soon after exposure. Another, older method for developing fingerprints is silver nitrate. Because silver nitrate had to be applied as an aqueous solution, it could not be used where water could damage the surface, which limited its use. A vast improvement on silver nitrate is physical developer, a silver-based product that contains a reducing agent. It can be used on similar surfaces to silver nitrate but it can also be used on surfaces that have been wet. Perhaps the most popular chemical method of fingerprint visualization is ninhydrin, an excellent reagent for developing fingerprint images on porous surfaces such as paper. Ninhydrin is sprayed directly onto a surface and reacts with any amino acids present in the fingerprint to form a colored compound, Ruhemann's Purple. At room temperature, it may take a couple of hours for prints to show up and weak prints may take more than a day. Heating the surface to about 100°C speeds up the reaction.

In 1982, Japanese scientists were experimenting with a cyanoacrylate ester that they had used to make a new type of glue. They heated some of the glue in a hood (fume cupboard); when they came back later, they found that fingerprints on glassware in the hood had become visible. The cyanoacrylate fumes had condensed preferentially on the fingerprint ridges – and so Super Glue® fuming was born. Today, many forensic science laboratories use tanks in which Super Glue® fuming can be done on many different types of objects. There are portable wands that can be used to fume small areas, and kits have been developed that can fume the inside of an automobile. The whitish prints visualized by cyanoacrylate are rock-hard and nearly impossible to remove. This is a great advantage over other chemical methods of fingerprint development because the fumed prints can then be treated with powders or other chemicals to increase the contrast between the print and the surface upon which it is found. If this secondary treatment doesn't work, it can be wiped away and another method tried.

Around the time that cyanoacrylate fuming was being developed, it was also discovered that fingerprint residues contain several substances that fluoresce when exposed to certain wavelengths of light. One problem is that the concentrations of these substances are usually low and thus very strong light sources are needed to provide enough energy to induce fluorescence. The first attempts to observe native fluorescence from fingerprints employed an argon-ion laser – some components of fingerprints fluoresce when exposed to this greenish light. However, even lasers cannot cause fluorescence in many fingerprints because the fluorescing materials are too sparse. After cyanoacrylate fuming was developed, forensic scientists took advantage of the near indestructibility of the fumed prints to treat the images with liquid fluorescent dyes, such as Rhodamine 6G. This dye absorbs green argon laser light and fluoresces, emitting yellow light. Since laser fingerprint development was pioneered, lasers have been replaced by other light sources, powerful lamps that use filters to shine one wavelength of light on a fingerprint. Rhodamine 6G has become one of the most popular methods of fingerprint development in forensic science laboratories today.

Comparison of fingerprints

The purpose of developing or visualizing latent fingerprints is to be able to compare them to fingerprint images taken from an individual who is a suspect in a criminal investigation. Known fingerprints are collected from a subject on a ten-print card, widely used to gather known fingerprints, which has a box for the rolled print of each finger and space for further information about the suspect. To collect the print, each finger is rolled in printer's ink from cuticle to cuticle and then rolled out into the proper box on the card, starting with the right thumb and proceeding to the right little finger in the top row and the left thumb through the left little finger on the bottom row. Below these ten blocks are spaces for tap prints, in which the four fingers of each hand are tapped in the printer's ink and into the proper block on the card. Tap prints are also made of each thumb.

To identify a particular person from their fingerprints, a complete set of inked fingerprints is taken and sent to a database such as the National Automated Fingerprint Identification System (**NAFIS**), which is used by the police services in England and Wales. It is based on the original **Henry system**. The Henry system uses several methods of classifying prints, each based on a different set of characteristics. Letter and number symbols are used to describe the type of each classification and the end result looks like a fraction with a series of numbers and letters in the numerator and denominator. Unfortunately, few crime scenes yield complete sets of fingerprints. More likely, there are just one or two and even they may be partial prints; that is, with part of the pattern missing. Partial prints can be matched to a known print if enough ridges are present. When the fingerprint examiner determines that there are sufficient points (friction ridge details) present in the unknown scene print and a known print, then an identification of the unknown can be made.

Until a few years ago, many countries had standards that set forth the number of points a fingerprint examiner had to find in a known and unknown print to be able to declare that an identification had been made. In some countries, the minimum number of points was ten; in others, it was twelve or sixteen, and so on. When there are many standards for the same identification, there is no standard, so, in 1990, the membership of the International Association for Identification, an umbrella group for experts including fingerprint examiners, declared that, henceforth, there would be no standard minimum number of points for identification but, instead, each examiner would determine how many points would be necessary.

There are three levels of friction ridge details:

- **Level 1 details**: the general features and pattern (for example, ulnar loops) of the fingerprint. These cannot be used for individualization but can be used to exclude a print from comparison.
- **Level 2 details**: particular ridges, such as endings or bifurcations. These minutiae enable individualization of an unknown print. What is important is not that the known and unknown prints contain the same number of each type of ridge, but that each detail is in the same place relative to other ridges in each print. In this sense, it is like comparing two samples of handwriting, where the individual characteristics lie not in the fact that the known and unknown contain the same number of "a"s and "e"s, but that the specific shapes and sizes of each letter are the same in each sample.
- **Level 3 details**: the minute imperfections in a print such as cuts, scars, edge shapes, and even sweat gland pores. These can only be seen under a microscope. These minutiae are so unusual that their presence in the known and unknown print almost ensures individuality. It should be noted, however, that the presence of many of these features depends upon how good the image of the print is. Some methods of fingerprint visualization are better at showing level 3 details than others and this must be taken into account when comparing prints.

Automated Fingerprint Identification Systems (AFIS and IAFIS)

The development of high-powered, easy-to-use, and readily available computers has had a profound effect on mankind, and it is no surprise that they have affected forensic science. One of the most dramatic advances that has been facilitated by computers is the automated search process for fingerprints. Prior to the development of computerized searching systems, it was impossible for law enforcement agencies to search vast data sets of ten-print fingerprint cards. In the beginning, they proceeded very slowly in using computers for this task. This was because computers with sufficient memory capacity to hold large databases of fingerprints were available only at great expense. In addition, the technology for faithfully capturing fingerprint images was rudimentary. When AFIS systems first came out, single fingerprints from crime scenes had to be enlarged and then the major ridges traced so the quality was good enough for the computers to scan them for searching. A standard format for storing fingerprint data was developed by the FBI with the help of the National Institute for Standards and Technology (NIST) and the National Crime Information Center (NCIC). Unfortunately, the companies that developed the hardware and software for conducting the searches did not use standard protocols and it was difficult to share data among users of different systems. In 1999, the FBI implemented a new automated system called the Integrated Automated Fingerprint Identification System (IAFIS). This is an entirely digital system that compares a person's set of ten fingerprints against a database of millions of sets of prints in a matter of a few minutes. In addition, it can search the database for a single latent print developed from a crime scene. All scanned fingerprints can now be digitally enhanced to improve clarity. The problem of incompatibility between different searching systems is being solved by the development of a new generation of workstations that are able to input fingerprints from all of the systems that are commercially available today. When these workstations are fully developed, law enforcement agents can search local, state, and national databases simultaneously. AFIS systems operate by anchoring the position of a fingerprint and searching the database using two types of ridges: bifurcations and ridge endings. The database is queried to find prints with the same number of these ridges in the same relative positions. The most likely candidates can be displayed for direct comparison.

Firearms

This section describes the analysis of firearms evidence. This is a large area of forensic analysis that covers such topics as associating bullets and cartridges with individual weapons, the ability of a weapon to fire, distance of firing measurements, directions and angles of firing, and questions about whether a person recently fired a weapon. In this book, only the part of firearms analysis that is concerned with matching bullets and cartridge cases to particular weapons will be discussed. A word about terminology is in order: people use the terms "bullets," "cartridges," "ammo," "round," and so on indiscriminately and imprecisely. Basically, a cartridge consists of the **cartridge case**, which holds the **gunpowder** (smokeless powder), and the **bullet**. The bullet is fired when the gunpowder burns and the cartridge case is left behind.

A **toolmark** is a scratch or other microscopic marking left by the action of a tool on an object. Examples of toolmarks include the microscopic impressions left by the blade of a wire cutter on the end of a cut wire, or the scrapings of the edge of a screwdriver left on a door jamb during an attempted break-in. A major part of firearms identification involves the analysis of toolmarks. With many weapons, a tool is used to ream out the barrel. These toolmarks are then transferred to the surface of a bullet that is fired through the barrel. Other markings are left on cartridges as the bullet is fired. These markings were also made by tools that made the parts of the weapon. The term "forensic ballistics" is often used as a synonym for firearms examinations but is somewhat of a misnomer, because **ballistics** is the study of projectiles in motion. Projectiles can range from bullets to baseballs to rocket ships. Firearms examiners are interested in ballistics, and it is a part of their knowledge, because they must understand the behavioral characteristics of bullets and shotgun pellets as they are fired by a weapon and reach their target. There are a huge number of different types of firearms for sale today in the US and elsewhere. Classifying them by type is not an exact science and there are many hybrid weapons. However, firearms examiners generally place weapons in one of five categories:

- **Pistols**: also sometimes called handguns because they were originally designed to be operated with one hand. Pistols are, in turn, divided into two subcategories:

  - **Revolvers**: pistols that contain a revolving cylinder with chambers that hold individual cartridges. As the weapon is cocked, the next chamber comes into line with the firing pin and barrel. After the bullet is fired, the cartridge remains in the cylinder and must be manually removed.
  - **Self-loading**: pistols usually loaded with a magazine that contains a number of bullets. This is loaded into the grip of the gun and the bullets are fed into the firing chamber by a spring-loading mechanism. The cartridges are extracted and ejected from the chamber manually after firing.

- **Rifles**: similar to pistols but made to be operated with two hands. There are a large number of different types of rifles, ranging from single shot to automatic rifles.
- **Machine guns**: fully automatic weapons that obtain their ammunition from magazines or belts. These weapons have heavy recoil when fired and cannot be safely fired by holding even with two hands but must have a fixed mounting.
- **Submachine guns**: like machine guns but designed to be hand-held.

- **Shotguns**: differ from the other four types of weapons in that they do not fire bullets. Instead, they fire small, usually round, pellets called "shot." Usually nine to ten pieces of shot are fired from a cartridge. Because shotguns do not fire bullets, they are not rifled.

In American football, when a quarterback throws the ball to a receiver, he lets the ball fall off his fingertips as he throws, imparting spin to the ball along its long axis. This spinning motion helps cut air resistance and keeps the ball on its intended trajectory. The consequences of the failure to impart spin to a projectile are put to advantage by a knuckleball pitcher in baseball. The pitcher deliberately throws the ball without spin, using his knuckles to grip the ball. Without spin, the ball is subject to air resistance and will travel towards the batter along an unpredictable trajectory, making the ball much harder to hit. The batter doesn't know where the ball is going and neither does the catcher, who will often be unable to catch a knuckleball. When someone fires a weapon at a target, they would like to ensure that the bullet has the best chance of landing where it is aimed. So, the bullet must be made to spin on its long axis as it emerges from the barrel of the weapon, which is accomplished by incorporating rifling in the barrel of the weapon.

Rifling is similar to a series of hills and valleys: the valleys are **grooves** and the hills between **lands**. Rifling consists of a series of lands and grooves. When a barrel is manufactured, a tool such as a rifling button or gang broach is used to dig spiral grooves into the inner surface of the barrel. Between each groove is a raised area, the land. There may be an odd or even number of lands and grooves and from two to nine of each. The number of lands and grooves, the direction of their twist through the barrel (clockwise or anti-clockwise), and the angle of twist are all class characteristics that can give valuable information to the firearms examiner about the manufacturer and model of the weapon.

The cutting surfaces of the broach or button that makes the lands and grooves contain microscopic imperfections that are the result of the tool used to manufacture it. These microscopic markings are transferred to the surfaces of the lands and grooves during the manufacture of the barrel. When the bullet is fired, it will pick up not only the lands and grooves but also the microscopic imperfections. These usually appear as tiny striations (or **stria**) in the lands and grooves. If the proper size ammunition is used in a rifled weapon, the bullet will expand due to the heat of the gunpowder being ignited. It will expand into the grooves and follow them like a track as it leaves the barrel. Because the grooves spiral through the barrel, the bullet will spin. Each land in the barrel digs a groove in the side of the bullet and each groove in the barrel will become a land in the bullet. Thus, the number of lands and grooves, and the angle and direction of their twist, can be determined by examining the fired bullet. The lands and grooves of the bullet will reflect the stria present in the barrel's lands and grooves. See Figure 15

Figure 15 A photomicrograph of a bullet showing lands, grooves, and stria

for a photomicrograph of a part of a bullet showing lands, grooves, and stria.

Cartridge cases are made of brass and come in a variety of shapes to suit different types of firearms. Like bullets, cartridge cases may have cannelures (grooves) impressed into the surface, which prevent the bullet from being pushed too far down into the cartridge. The heads of some cartridges have markings stamped into the surface, which reveal the manufacturer and/or the caliber. Other markings on cartridges are those made by extractors and ejectors (in self-loading pistols), firing-pin impressions, and breechblock markings.

The oldest recorded propellant is black powder. This was invented by the Chinese around the tenth century BCE and used for signals and fireworks. Black powder is a mixture of fine particles of charcoal, sulfur, and saltpeter. Formulations vary but saltpeter is always the major component. Even though smokeless powders have entirely replaced black powder as a commercial propellant, it is still used by battle reenactors and fans of old weapons. Black powder produces lots of smoke that can reveal the position of the shooter. Smokeless powder, developed in the late nineteenth century, emits much less smoke. Smokeless powders consist of cotton lint or wood pulp impregnated with a strong acid, and some also contain the powerful explosive nitroglycerine. It is important to note that smokeless powders do not explode inside a cartridge, but combust. Since the combustion is occurring in a closed space, it has the force of an explosion.

In 1807, a Scottish clergyman, Alexander John Forsyth, discovered a shock-sensitive explosive, mercury fulminate. This type of explosive will detonate if it is struck or shocked and will also be set off by a spark. By 1840, cartridges were being manufactured that contained mercury fulminate inside the head of the cartridge as the primer. At first, the primer was inserted inside the rim of the cartridge. A small pin protruded from the back of the rim, which, when struck by the hammer, struck the primer, detonating it. The detonation caused the powder inside the cartridge to ignite. By 1850, this system was replaced by a simpler one, in which the primer was inserted into a tiny cup inside the center of the cartridge head and the firing pin was mounted on the end of the hammer. When it struck the cup of the primer, it compressed the primer and detonated it. The flame produced by the detonation escaped through a hole in the cup and ignited the propellant. When gunshot residue taken from the hands of a shooter is analyzed, the examiner looks for particles of antimony, lead, and barium from the primer.

Examination of bullets and cartridge cases

Bullets and cartridge cases recovered from crime scenes may contain significant amounts of trace evidence. This evidence is first analyzed by a trace evidence examiner. Trace evidence found on the surfaces of fired bullets can include hairs, fibers, paint, metal, and tissue. Cartridge cases may bear readable finger-prints, as well as trace evidence.

The proper collection of known materials for comparison with crime scene bullets and cartridge cases is crucial. The suspect weapon must be test-fired with ammunition that is as close as possible to that from the crime scene. Recovery of cartridge cases is easy: in revolvers, they stay in the cylinder; in pistols, they are ejected near the source of firing. Recovery of bullets is not quite as simple. Originally, traps made of cotton or other types of wadding were used to capture test-fired bullets. These had to be very thick to cope with high-powered ammunition and it could be a tedious chore to find the bullet. Some types of wadding were abrasive and could change the markings on the bullets. Today, most crime laboratories use a large, deep, stainless steel tank filled with water. These tanks can be eight feet long and nearly as deep. The bottom of the tank is cone-shaped, so that a test-fired bullet will roll to the point of the cone, where it is recovered in a small basket. Enough water will stop almost any bullet and will not damage its surface.

Fired bullets have both class and individual characteristics. Class characteristics include the number of lands and grooves and the angle and direction of twist. These data alone can give clues as to the make and model of the weapon. The microscopic stria imparted to the land and groove surfaces are potentially individual characteristics and are always compared using a **comparison microscope**. A comparison microscope is two microscopes in one, joined by a **comparison bridge**. One bullet is mounted on the stage of each microscope. The comparison bridge permits simultaneous viewing of both objects, one with each eye. The bullets can be rotated so that a land or groove on one bullet can be compared with all the lands or grooves on the other.

An important question with respect to the comparison of bullets or any other toolmarks is: "how many corresponding stria must be found before a firearms examiner can declare that the two bullets were fired from the same weapon?" There is no absolute standard; two firearms examiners may have different opinions as to what constitutes a match and may reach different conclusions about a bullet comparison. (This is generally true of all pattern evidence; there is no general agreement about the number of corresponding characteristics there must be between a known and unknown piece of evidence.) Just because two bullets were fired from the same weapon doesn't mean that the stria will always match. For example, rust may build up inside the barrel of a weapon and the stria on a bullet may be due mainly to rust. As bullets are fired from such a gun, rust particles are removed and the stria will change. Even if rust isn't a problem, repeated firings of a weapon will cause changes in the stria pattern, especially with metal-jacketed bullets. Imperfections in the surface of the jacket can impart stria to the barrel of the gun and remove some that are already there. After fifty or so firings, the stria of the fiftieth bullet may not match the first. Some weapons have interchangeable barrels: this can clearly cause problems if the barrel is changed after the crime scene bullet was fired but before the weapon is test-fired.

Cartridges can yield the same types of information as bullets. The examiner will attempt to determine the type of weapon used. If a suspect weapon is present, it can be determined if the cartridge was fired by that weapon. A number of markings on cartridges that help make these associations include: stria from firing-pin impressions, extractor and ejector markings (except in revolvers), breechblock markings, and, sometimes, chamber markings. There are a few stria on the surface of firing pins; when the pin strikes the head of the cartridge, these are transferred to the cartridge. When a bullet is fired, the cartridge recoils back towards the shooter. A block of metal, the breech, stops the cartridge from hitting the shooter. This block contains stria, which are transferred to the surface of the head of the cartridge. The extractor grabs the cartridge so that it can be ejected from the chamber and make room for another live round.

Handwriting

A **questioned document** is any written or printed communication whose source or authenticity is in doubt. The document doesn't have to be written on paper and in ink: questioned documents have been written on the sides of houses, mirrors, and tables; in ink, blood, paint, or even lipstick. Questioned documents include forged passports, currency, draft cards, and driver's licenses. Any commerce between people that involves a document has the potential for fraud, forgery, alteration, counterfeiting, or theft. Questioned document examiners must know a great deal about writing, printing, typewriting, inks, papers, and methods of altering or obliterating writing.

The analysis of handwriting is the oldest and most challenging type of questioned document examination. Signatures notwithstanding, the increasing use of computers in everyday life has decreased the use of handwritten documents in personal and business discourse; nevertheless, handwriting analysis remains a classic illustration of the principles and issues arising from pattern evidence. It has been traditionally considered individual evidence, but a number of recent court cases have successfully challenged the admissibility of handwriting comparisons for identification purposes.

Questioned document examiners are often called upon to determine the authorship of a handwritten document. This means that known handwriting samples, often called **exemplars**, must be obtained from the suspected author. To make a correct comparison, the exemplar must be similar in all controllable aspects to the unknown writing. These aspects include the type of writing instrument, the type of writing (printing, script), the type of paper (lined, unlined), and the time. Handwriting changes with time, so it is important that the questioned writing and the known writing are collected at about the same time. There are two types of exemplars: **requested** and **nonrequested writings**. Each has advantages and drawbacks and is used under different circumstances.

Requested exemplars are sought by an investigator or may be ordered by a court. There is no question of authenticity in these circumstances so admissibility is usually not an issue. When exemplars are requested, the circumstances are arranged so that the conditions of collections are as similar to those of the unknown sample as possible. For example, unless it is known for certain that the questioned document was made when the writer was in an uncomfortable position, the subject should be made as comfortable as possible, with the best possible chair, table, and lighting. Likewise, the same type and color of writing instrument should be used (if the questioned document was written with a blue gel pen, so should the exemplar), and the paper should be of the same type (for example, lined or unlined) for both exemplar and unknown.

The exemplar is always taken under dictation. The subject is not shown the questioned document and is not allowed to copy it, but document examiners recommend that it is often helpful to include some phrases and sentences from the document in the dictation. This is especially important where there are misspellings or mistakes in grammar in the questioned document, as the subject may repeat these mistakes in the exemplar. Dictation also reduces the opportunities to alter the handwriting: the act of handwriting is subconscious and altering one's handwriting on purpose takes conscious effort. If a passage is dictated, the subject must listen to the words and write them down. This makes it harder to concentrate on disguising the handwriting.

Sufficient exemplars should be taken. Requesting long passages of handwriting will ensure that a representative sample is being gathered and helps to uncover attempts to disguise the handwriting. As the length of the passage increases, it becomes increasingly difficult to maintain deliberately altered writing. Eventually, most people will lapse back into their habitual ways of writing. Exemplars should be taken in context. If the questioned document is a check, the subject should be asked to fill out a number of checks (perhaps ten to twenty) for various amounts. If the questioned document is a signature, the subject should be asked to write their signature many times on documents similar to the questioned document.

There are inherent disadvantages to requested writings: the foremost is that the request calls attention to the fact that the subject's handwriting is at issue, and the subject may be tempted to alter it. The request may also cause the subject to be apprehensive or nervous, both of which conditions can cause unintended alterations in handwriting.

Non-requested writing consists of documents written by the subject for purposes other than the questioned document case. They may be documents written in the normal course of business, correspondence, or items such as diaries that are likely to represent the writer's true handwriting. The writer did not write the document with the idea that it may be used as an exemplar and so no emphasis or attention is directed at the writing.

Even though non-requested writings represent the writer's true penmanship, there are disadvantages to this type of exemplar. Unless the writings clearly identify the author, it may be difficult to introduce them as evidence in court. Also, the non-requested writing will probably not bear any resemblance to the questioned document and may not contain enough of the same words or phrases, making comparison more difficult. It is also important that the exemplar and the questioned document are of about the same age. Many questioned document examiners prefer that exemplars are a combination of requested and non-requested samples.

Questioned document examiners follow a few simple rules when comparing handwriting:

- No two people have identical handwriting.
- There is a natural variation in a person's writing.
- No one writes the same letter or number exactly the same way twice (one reason why large samples of writings are needed so that the examiner may observe the range of variation in an individual's).
- No one single writing characteristic is so unique by itself that it will individualize handwriting.
- There is no set number of characteristics that must be present for an examiner to identify the author of a questioned document.

As with any type of evidence comparison, there must be a sufficient number of similarities between the known and unknown and no unexplainable differences. Like many types of evidence, handwriting has class and individual characteristics. Document examiners must make sure their conclusions about the authenticity or authorship of a questioned document are based on individual characteristics. For example, the slant of the writing is generally a class characteristic, whereas unusual flourishes at the end of words, or ornate capital letters, are individual characteristics. When a questioned document examiner focuses on particular letters or letter combinations, they often create a chart that shows several instances of these letters in both the known and unknown writing samples to demonstrate the natural variation in the writer's style and display the similarity of the characteristic in both documents to the jury at a trial. Signatures can be especially problematic for a questioned document examiner: a questioned document may consist solely of one signature. For example, a fraudulent check may have only the payee, the amount, and the signature on it, and only the signature identifies the author. As discussed earlier, the appearance of signatures is very sensitive to their context, so the exemplars must be taken under conditions that approximate those under which the questioned document was made. There are numerous cases in which a forger attempts to mimic or forge another person's handwriting and very often the forgery will be a signature. The forger will obtain someone else's authentic signature and practice copying it. Unless the forger is expert, attempts at forgery can usually be uncovered by careful examination of the writing. Signs of forgery include differences in line quality (thickness or smoothness), connecting strokes, pen lifts, starts and stops, and retouching. Another common type of forgery is tracing, which can be accomplished in several ways. For example, the forger may put a piece of tracing paper over the document and trace the writing using a sharp object; the tracing is then used as a template for the forged writing; or a new document may be placed over the original and the writing directly traced onto it. Tracings are usually not hard to detect: the line quality invariably suffers, often appearing uneven, with a quality of having been "drawn," or appearing to have been written very slowly – which it usually has. A third type of fraud occurs when a forger doesn't bother to duplicate the writing of the original author but instead uses their own, but disguised, handwriting to write the document. The forger is counting on the fact that the original writing is not available to those people who would read or act on the documents.

Hair

What is hair?

Hair is an outgrowth of the **epidermis**, or outer layer of the skin. It is found only in mammals. The epidermis contains follicles, which are the structures from which hairs originate and grow. When hair begins to grow, its outer covering is soft. When it reaches the top of the skin, the outer layer begins to harden into **keratin**, which is made of proteins. Inside the follicle, where the hair is growing, it is enervated by blood vessels, which provide nourishment and which exchange materials between blood and the inside of the hair. Anything that is ingested by the person, such as food, drugs, or poisons, will eventually be incorporated into the growing region of the hair. When the hair reaches the surface of the skin and keratinizes, it is essentially dead. It is no longer in contact with blood vessels and doesn't exchange anything with its biologic environment. This means that whatever substances were absorbed by the growing part of the hair will remain there. Thus, when hair grows, it is really being "pushed up" by the growing part of the hair in the follicle. It is analogous to the size of a stack of dinner plates growing taller by continuously adding more plates to the bottom of the stack. The plates on the top aren't getting bigger, they are being pushed out and up by the ones being added from below. If a person ingests cocaine, for example, some of it will be absorbed into the growing region of the person's hair. As this section of the hair gets pushed up and out from the follicle, the cocaine remains in that section of the hair until the hair is cut or falls out. This is why drug analysis is being performed increasingly on hair. The hair retains some of the drug each time the person uses it. Unlike urine analysis, which provides only a snapshot of the drugs in a person's body, hair analysis provides a history. Head hair grows approximately one-half inch per month. This can be used to estimate the time when a drug or other substance was ingested.

Is it possible to determine if a hair has been forcibly removed? In some cases, it is obvious that hair has been pulled out. Some, but not all forcibly removed hair will have follicle cells clinging to the hair. Some may actually have blood on the root. This would be especially true if the hair was still growing. If the hair was in a resting phase when pulled, it may not have any of the follicle sheath on it because bulbous roots of the hair in this phase are not tightly held in the follicle. The amount of cellular material on the root depends on how fast the hair was pulled. If the hair is pulled quickly, the chances of finding cells from the follicle are increased.

Hair gets its native color from a pigment called **melanin**. As hair grows, special cells called **melanocytes** produce granules of melanin. There are two types of melanin. One is dark brown and the other is lighter, almost blond. Under the influence of genetic instructions, these two types of melanin are present in various combinations, densities, and distributions, giving rise to the natural hair colors in the human population. Melanin granules are dispersed throughout the middle layer of the hair (the cortex). When hair is dyed, the melanin does not take up the dye. Instead, the dye coats the surface of the hair.

The structure of hair

Hair is not a homogeneous solid or hollow tube. In some ways, it resembles a lead pencil. A pencil has three layers: the outer paint, the thick middle layer made of wood, and the inner shaft of graphite. Hair also contains three layers. The cross section of a human scalp hair is shown in Figure 16. The outer layer of hair is called the **cuticle**. It is made of keratin, the same substance that makes up fingernails and toenails in humans and horns in other animals. It is hard and inert. In some animals, such as the porcupine, the cuticle is so rigid and thick that the hair is a sharp needle that can be used as a weapon. In humans, the cuticle is very thin and is made up of overlapping scales like shingles on a roof.

The middle layer of hair is the **cortex.** In human hairs, this is the largest layer. It takes up more than half the diameter of the hair, like the wood layer in a pencil. The cortex is made up of spindle-shaped cells. The melanocytes, described above as responsible for the hair's color, are dispersed throughout the cortex. These granules are generally not spaced in an even pattern but, instead, are often found in clumps. They vary from person to person in size and shape as well as distribution. The cortex

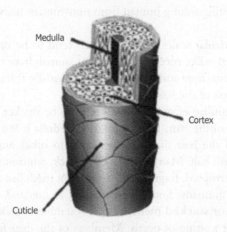

Medulla

Cortex

Cuticle

Figure 16 The microscopic structure of human hair

also contains **cortical fusi**, small bubble-like structures. **Ovoid bodies**, which look like large pigment granules, may also be present in the cortex. Their function is not known. They do not exhibit a pattern but appear irregularly within the cortex.

The inner layer of the hair shaft is the **medulla**. In humans, it tends to be of narrow diameter. In scalp hairs, the medulla can range from totally absent to continuous, with fragmented (mostly absent) or interrupted (mostly present) in between. See Figure 16.

Human v. non-human hairs

Many animals possess three different types of hair. The first are called **guard hairs**. These are firm hairs that are used for microscopic comparison. The rest of the animal's coat is filled in with **fur hairs**. These are relatively featureless and do not provide much information about the type of animal. Finally, there are **whiskers**. These are also relatively featureless.

There are a number of microscopic characteristics that can be useful in distinguishing human from non-human hairs:

- The cuticular scales of human hairs tend to be unorganized and overlap like roof shingles. Other animals have more organized, patterned scales. The cuticle is usually thicker relative to the rest of the hair in other animals.
- The medullae of other animals tend to be thicker relative to the rest of the hair. In humans, the medulla is less than one-third of the hair diameter, whereas, in other animals, it is more than half. Many animals have thick, continuous medullae. Interrupted, fragmented, and absent medullae are present only in humans. Some animals such as cats and mice have **ladder** or **stacked** medullae that resemble a stack of dinner plates or a string of pearls. Members of the deer family have medullae that look like fine latticework.

Collection and comparison of hair evidence

In a typical case, hairs from the perpetrator and/or victim are discovered at the scene of a crime. The goal of the examination is to determine if these hairs of unknown source can be associated with the possible source. Except in the most unusual circumstances, hairs are class evidence and it is not possible to a degree of reasonable scientific certainty to conclude that unknown hairs came from a particular person. Moreover, if known and unknown hairs are similar in their structural characteristics, it is not possible to assign any numerical probability that the hairs came from the same source. This is because there is no taxonomy that would permit classification of a hair by the condition or types of cuticle, cortex, and medulla. These hair characteristics occur on a type of continuum; there are no discrete types that would give rise to population frequencies.

As with other types of evidence, the collection of known samples is important. In the majority of cases, either head or pubic (or both) hairs are left as evidence at crime scenes. It is important to get a sufficient number of known hairs and they must represent the head or pubic area as a whole. At least two dozen hairs are needed for comparisons. Fifty is better. They must be combed and pulled to ensure that hairs in all stages of growth are represented. The known sample must contain hairs from areas that have been treated. This includes dyeing, braiding, bleaching, graying, etc. There are natural variations of morphological characteristics of hairs within the same head or other area of the body. There must be enough known samples present so that the hair examiner is aware of the degree of variation. One of the reasons that hair cannot be individualized is that the degree of variation within one head of hair often exceeds the variation between two people's hair.

Hairs are mounted on microscope slides and immersed in a suitable liquid that enables the examiner to see through the cuticle into the inner layers of the hair. The cuticle has a refractive index of about 1.50. Suitable known refractive index liquids can be used, as can glycerin (RI=1.475). The microscope should be able to provide magnification of 25-200 power. A comparison microscope is ideal so that known and unknown hairs can be viewed together. Scale casts should also be taken of some of the knowns and unknowns.

Various charts are used by hair examiners to record the data about the known and unknown hair. There is no standard set of data that must be collected. The examiner typically collects data about the hair sample as a whole including lengths, diameters, coloring, diseases, and treatments. In addition, specific information is noted for the root, shaft, and tip. Characteristics of the medulla are noted including its diameter, continuity, and color. The cortex is examined for the presence and distribution of color granules, ovoid bodies, and cortical fusi.

On the basis of the comparison of unknown hairs, there are three possible conclusions that a hair examiner can reach. If there are sufficient common characteristics between the knowns and unknowns and there are no unexplainable significant differences, then the hair examiner can conclude that the unknown hairs could have originated from the person who provided the known samples. If the known and unknown samples exhibit significant differences that exceed the range of variation within a set of hairs, then the conclusion would be that the known donor could not have been the source of the unknown hairs. If there are some similarities between the known and unknown but there are also some slight variations, then no conclusion about the association can be reached.

What can be determined from the morphology of hair?

Even if there are no known samples with which to compare unknown hairs, there is a good deal of information that can be gained from the analysis of the unknowns by themselves.

Unfortunately, there are a number of misconceptions about what can be reliably determined.

- **Age**: Age cannot be determined from the examination of hair. The fact that hair is gray doesn't mean that the person is old. The only hair that can be differentiated by age is the very fine hair called **lanugo** that newborns are born with.
- **Gender**: At one time, perhaps fifty years ago, people may have concluded that long hair was female. If hair spray was present, it must be female. One would be tempted to say that only females dyed their hair. Neither of these is true today, if they ever were. The only reliable determinant for gender in hair is a DNA analysis to see if the "Y" (male) chromosome is present.
- **Race**: There are some racial characteristics of hair that show up if the person has fairly pure racial ancestry. These include different hair diameters, cross-sectional shapes, thickness of cuticle, and distribution of pigments. As intermarriages take place, these characteristics tend to become less pronounced.
- **Color**: The determination of whether hair, has been dyed or bleached, or if it is the natural color of the hair, is fairly routine. Dyeing tends to coat the hair, almost like paint. Bleach will wash out most or all of the color in the color granules.

Over the past twenty years in the US, there have been a number of criminal cases involving the analysis of human hair where the examiner overstated the value of morphological hair comparison. In other cases, a hair examiner made correct conclusions that hairs are class evidence and that a suspect could have been the source of hairs obtained from a crime scene, but that an unknown number of other people could also have been the source. Many years later, when DNA typing of hairs was developed (see below) and hair evidence was reanalyzed, it was found that the suspect was not the source of the hair from the scene. These types of cases have led to a marked decrease in cases where hairs are compared morphologically at all. Many crime laboratories have simply stopped analyzing hair. This is unfortunate because, as we have seen, a good deal of useful information can be gained from the comparison of hairs, and properly interpreted and communicated results of hair comparisons should not lead to miscarriages of justice.

DNA and hair

Like other biological material, hair contains DNA. Cellular DNA is found only in the root of the hair. If a hair falls out on its own or is forcibly removed, the root is often present. There may also be scalp tissue clinging to the root if the hair is forcibly removed. DNA from the root can be extracted, amplified, and analyzed as with other nuclear DNA. If a hair is cut or falls out without the root, then there is no nuclear DNA. There is, however, another type of DNA present in all hair cells, even those that are not part of the root. This is mitochondrial DNA. Nuclear DNA can be used to associate hairs with a particular individual to a very high degree of certainty that is tantamount to individualization. As discussed in Chapter 9, mitochondrial DNA cannot be individualized. There are not enough differences in mitochondrial DNA between people. In fact, all offspring from the same mother have the same mitochondrial DNA.

Fingerprints, firearms and toolmarks, and handwriting are all types of pattern evidence, forming patterns although of different types. Fingerprint patterns are the arrangement of ridges on the last joint of the fingers and thumbs. They form during gestation and are unchanged, except for size, throughout life. Firearms and toolmarks patterns are scratches and other markings that are imparted to bullets, cartridges, and the surfaces of objects that have been subject to tools. These markings change as the gun or tool is used repeatedly. Handwriting develops during early childhood as it is taught in school. It soon becomes internalized and is a function of the writer's habits, dexterity, and mental state.

All these pattern types are considered individual evidence; under the proper conditions, each can be associated with a particular source. This makes them very valuable as evidence. All have been admitted in courts throughout the world for more than a hundred years. However, all of them are now being scrutinized, because of a perceived or actual lack of scientific foundation to their conclusions.

11
Ethics and forensic science

Because the work of forensic scientists can have significant effects upon the criminal justice system as a whole, they must maintain high standards of personal and professional integrity. In other words, forensic scientists must have high standards of ethics. Ethics is part of philosophy. It is concerned with actions that are right or wrong and the outcomes of these actions. The concept of right and wrong varies within societies and groups within a society. Most major endeavors have their own particular code of ethics. Knowledge of professional ethics provides the foundation for the development of acceptable behavior throughout one's professional life.

Forensic scientists face two types of ethical issues in their work life. The first set of issues arises because, first of all, forensic scientists are scientists. There are ethical dilemmas and questions that arise among all scientists, and most forensic scientists see themselves as professional scientists above all else. The second set of ethical questions arises because forensic scientists have a unique relationship, as scientists, with the justice system. This is especially true in the justice systems in the United Kingdom and the United States, which are adversarial in nature. Each case has two *sides* that are pitted against one another in the courtroom. The forensic scientist, in trying to remain above the fray and apply their science in a neutral, unbiased way, is constantly being buffeted by the competing interests of each side in a case.

Among the potential ethical problems that can arise in the practice of forensic science, a few stand out for their frequency of occurrence and importance. These include the use of best scientific practices, employing validated methods of analysis, becoming an advocate for one side of a legal dispute, seeking personal gain or notoriety, and acting in a biased fashion. Some of these are discussed in more detail below.

Professional credentials

One of the most pervasive ethical problems that cuts across all scientific fields involves the establishment of professional credentials. Expert witnesses in general and scientists in particular are often called upon to demonstrate their credentials including education and experience. If an expert is hired by an attorney to provide advice to the client, the expert must convince the attorney that they are qualified to provide expert opinions. Likewise, when an expert witness is offered to the court, they must demonstrate their credentials to the judge. The attorney who wishes to employ an expert for advice or for expert testimony has the responsibility to verify that the expert actually possesses the education and experience that they claim to have. In a courtroom, it is the judge who makes the ultimate decision on whether a proffered expert witness will be permitted to offer testimony. There is very limited opportunity in a courtroom during a trial for either party or the judge to verify that the expert has the qualifications they claim. Thus, there is a temptation on the part of unscrupulous scientists and other experts to embellish their credentials to make themselves appear more qualified and thus more desirable as an expert witness or to be able to charge higher fees. All testimony in court is a matter of record and an expert who lies about their credentials is committing perjury. In today's internet environment, it is easier than ever to check out statements made by experts concerning their credentials. Nonetheless, the practice of inflating credentials continues to flourish because there is so little in the way of verification.

Professional development

A major ethical and professional requirement of being a good scientist is to remain current in one's field. This is especially true in the analysis of scientific evidence by forensic scientists. Some areas of forensic science, especially DNA analysis, change quite rapidly. If a forensic scientist is using outdated or invalidated methodology in the analysis of evidence, they may end up with incorrect or incomplete results. Thus, keeping up with developments in forensic science is an ethical necessity. There are a number of ways that forensic scientists can maintain currency in their field. They can and should keep up with the published research literature. This is the most efficient way of getting the latest information about the field. Of course, this means that they should concentrate on the most respected, peer-reviewed literature. In addition to journals, new text and reference books are arriving all the time and, although they are a bit dated when they are published, they contain more material presented more comprehensively than journals.

Another way of keeping current in forensic science, or any science for that matter, is to attend and participate in regional and national meetings where the latest research is presented and networking opportunities abound. Short courses and workshops are often available at these meetings so there are usually many opportunities for professional development and continuing education.

So where do ethical problems occur in the professional development and maintenance of currency in the field? It is one thing to have books, journals, and professional meetings available, but it is quite another to actually follow through and participate. A scientist can claim to have read the latest manuscripts and books, but how is that to be verified? There are also numerous instances of scientists registering for a meeting and even attending but, once there, they do not participate in the professional development activities but, instead, spend the days at the golf course or swimming pool. Instances of this seem to increase where meetings are held at prime resorts in the high season. In most cases, there are few or no checks or verifications that someone actually partook in the professional development aspects of a meeting or actually read the books and journals.

Laboratory analysis

Best laboratory practice in any science dictates that all analytical tests be written and validated and that there exist rigorous protocols for administrative and technical reviews of analyses and reports. Most forensic science laboratories follow these practices but there is little uniformity or consensus about how these procedures should be followed. The existence of approved analytical schemes and standard operating procedures does not guarantee that they will be rigorously followed by all scientists at all times. There have been several recent, high-profile instances of forensic scientist misconduct in laboratory analysis of evidence. Ethical violations occur when forensic scientists do not follow required procedures or when they use non-validated methods of analysis.

One of the major ethical issues in evidence analysis is the sufficiency of analysis. In forensic science, a scientist is duty bound to perform enough scientific testing to support the conclusions about the identity and association that are reached on the basis of the analysis. In most types of forensic evidence, there are no standards that define how much testing is enough or too much. If there is not a thorough and rigorous technical and administrative review of all evidence analyzed by every forensic examiner, the possibility of ethical violations exists. One example of how this plays out occurs where an examiner is faced with repetitive, basic testing of evidence such as bags of cannabis (marijuana). It would be easy to open the bags of plant material, sniff the contents, and then close the bags and report out that all of the tests were performed and the plant material was cannabis. It would be very difficult to uncover this violation of laboratory procedure. This practice of reporting out conclusions about evidence without examining it even has a name; it is called **dry-labbing** (see Chapter 1). There is anecdotal evidence that this practice may be widespread in certain forensic science laboratories.

Another unethical practice in some forensic science laboratories is "analyzing to the law." Certain types of evidence are controlled and/or described by statute. The field of illicit drugs is the best example. In some jurisdictions, a drug is defined specifically and some laws prescribe penalties for possession or distribution of a drug that depend upon the weight of the evidence. In cases where the weight of the evidence is very close to a penalty break point, it would be easy for the scientist to report out the weight just above or just below the limit, depending upon their bias towards the government or the defendant.

Ethics of reporting and interpretation

The culmination of all forensic analysis is a laboratory report. The marks of a "best practice" scientific laboratory report are completeness, thoroughness, and clarity. All testing should be described. Results and conclusions should be clearly stated and backed up by thorough analysis of the data. All data should be presented and error rates clearly and accurately disclosed. This is especially important in the case of reports of forensic analysis. Laboratory reports are often used by prosecutors to help determine what, if any, charges should be leveled against an accused person in a crime. Reports are often used by parties in a civil case to help determine damages and charges. Reports may be used as evidence themselves if the reporting scientist is not called into court to testify. The ethical problem with laboratory reports in the forensic science setting is that they are very often not as comprehensive and forthcoming as they should be. Many reports are very brief – little more than a certificate of analysis. They contain only a description of the evidence received and the results of the tests. They do not contain a description of the testing or how the conclusions were reached or any of the data. This makes it very difficult for a judge, jury, or attorneys to determine the validity of the testing or to question the findings of the report. A recent research study by the author of this book, of 421 redacted laboratory reports in the US, confirmed that most reports are not as complete as they should be.

The most critical part of the forensic science laboratory report is often the degree of association of evidence with a known source. This association is best illustrated with the various types of pattern evidence discussed in Chapter 10. In many cases involving fingerprints, toolmarks, handwriting, shoeprints, tire marks, etc., scientists have reached conclusions of individuality; the unknown evidence *came from* the same source as the known – for example, the fingerprint found on the gun was made by the left index finger of the accused. These types of comparisons give rise to terminology that has not been defined by consensus in the forensic science field and may mean different things to different scientists as well as to judges and juries. For example, the term "match," as in the known and unknown bullets matched, is a poorly defined term. It may mean that the bullets came from the same weapon or it may mean that they could have been fired from the same weapon. If the scientist cannot clearly and unambiguously define such terms as match, "similar to," "could not be eliminated as the source of," etc., then there is a significant risk of the trier of fact being misled about scientific evidence. This can be a serious violation of professional ethics.

Bias

Bias is a tendency to slant one's opinions or beliefs or practices towards or away from one of several possible points of view. Bias is very often subconscious. People do not realize that they are acting in a biased fashion, even when it is pointed out to them. One could argue that there is no such thing as an unbiased opinion – that everyone has a point of view that reflects their own vision and is thus always biased. Court decisions in many countries as well as some surprising verdicts in criminal trials have brought forward the issue of biased behavior and how it may affect forensic science. There is, of course, the most obvious example of bias in the forensic science context, where a scientist knowingly and willingly espouses conclusions about evidence that are biased in favor of one party or the other, without having evidence that these conclusions reflect scientific validity. There have been a number of well-known instances of biased conduct on the part of forensic scientists in the UK and the US.

There are other, more subtle types of bias that operate within many fields of science but which have been examined only recently for their influence on forensic science. One type of bias is called **situational** bias. This occurs in cases where a forensic science laboratory is part of a law enforcement agency such as a police department or prosecutor's office. In some cases, forensic scientists themselves are sworn police officers. In these situations, it is easy for a scientist to become biased towards the prosecution in a crime because the police department works hand in hand with the prosecutor's office in prosecuting people accused of crimes. These forensic examiners no longer see themselves as unbiased scientists, but instead are advocates for the department in which they work. It is for this reason that the US National Academy of Sciences called for administrative independence of forensic science laboratories from law enforcement agencies.

Another type of serious bias that is being studied in conjunction with forensic science is known as **observer bias** or **observer effects.** These are also known as **context**, **expectancy**, and **confirmation effects**. In the forensic science context, observer effects occur when the results and conclusions reached by forensic scientists in their evaluation of scientific evidence are influenced by extraneous knowledge: information that does not apply directly to the scientific inquiry being undertaken. Observer bias can go farther than just possessing extraneous knowledge. It can also include subconscious expectations and desires of the examiner. This bias can be manifested in the form of alterations in the wording of forensic science case results and conclusions to subtly favor the prosecution or defense. In some extreme cases, an examiner will fabricate evidence and provide false testimony because of bias. Observer bias can and does occur in virtually every area of forensic science but its potential for harm is arguably greatest in the pattern areas described in Chapter 10. Fingerprints, firearms and toolmarks, handwriting, and other types of pattern evidence, such as hairs, bite marks, blood spatter, and similar types of evidence, have one major characteristic in common: examiners are called upon to try to establish the source of the evidence by comparing it with known exemplars and uncovering "unique" characteristics. There is no backup data supplied by scientific instruments and no established taxonomy that would establish relative commonality or rarity of particular features, and thus no numerical basis for conclusions of an association. The examiner has only their knowledge, skills, aptitudes, and experience to draw upon. As such, any subtle or overt bias that creeps into the mind of the examiner can unwittingly (or not) influence the conclusions reached in a particular case.

Observer bias is a very well known phenomenon in cognitive psychology. It affects virtually every type of scientific inquiry and is recognized as pervasive by most responsible scientists, to the point where extraordinary measures such as double-blind testing and completely independent retesting are sometimes incorporated for the sole purpose of eliminating or at least minimizing bias. Even so, many forensic scientists believe that they are free of such biases. They claim to be aware of the possibility of observer bias and, thus alerted, are able to purge it from their minds and claim with great certainty that their personal beliefs and knowledge about a case have no bearing on their final conclusions. Indeed, freedom from bias is said to be one of the characteristics that define a forensic scientist. In spite of these beliefs, there is ample evidence from actual cases and some limited forensic science-specific research that has shown time and again that observer bias is prevalent and deeply rooted in forensic science. This collective state of mind that denies the existence of bias also inhibits production of the research that is needed to establish its prevalence and impact. Although general experiments in cognitive psychology can and do shed light on the issue of observer bias in the scientific community, research is needed in forensic science, using forensic scientists in real analysis situations to determine how bias affects their everyday work.

Practices that reflect bias

The "showup": single sample testing

Consider the situation of the identification of a possible crime suspect by a witness. There is usually a physical or photographic lineup whereby the witness is asked to pick out the suspect from a group of people who are similar in appearance, or from a group of photographs. This procedure is used to minimize the effects of observer bias. The witness is less likely to focus on one specific person because they are among a group of people. Now consider the typical forensic science laboratory case: Evidence is collected from a crime scene. A suspect is developed and/or a victim is identified. Evidence from the crime scene is submitted to the laboratory along with known samples from the suspect. For the forensic scientist, this suspect becomes the focus of the evidence analysis. There are no other possible suspects and thus no one to change the focus of the investigation. This sets up an almost unavoidable situation of observer bias. With the focus of the police investigation on this suspect and the forensic scientist in possession only of evidence from that suspect, the focus of the scientist will also be on that suspect and bias can easily creep in.

Domain-irrelevant information

Typically, when a forensic scientist in a laboratory receives evidence from a crime, they are also given ancillary data such as the type of crime, name of the suspect and victim, details of the crime, and how the particular evidence fits into the case. Much of this information may be irrelevant to the data needed to actually carry out the scientific examinations required by the case. The fact that the evidence in a case of fraud is a signature on a check and that the exemplar was submitted by someone who was seen cashing a similar check is irrelevant to the scientific examination of the handwriting characteristics that make up the signatures. Yet this information can have a significant effect on the conclusions reached by the examiner. Domain-irrelevant information varies from case to case and among forensic science disciplines. It could be argued, for example, that forensic pathologists need much more information about a case, in order to properly determine cause and manner of death, than would a firearms examiner who must determine if a bullet was fired from a particular weapon.

Selective reporting and reexamination

In some cases, a forensic scientist may be asked to perform analysis on evidence by an attorney who then tells the scientist not to create a report on the analysis or to report only certain aspects of the analysis. This is usually because the attorney doesn't like the conclusions reached by the scientist and wants to hide them from the other party. This is, of course, unethical behavior on the part of the attorney and the forensic scientist.

Confirmational bias

At the beginning of Chapter 10, a part of the Madrid, Spain, terrorist bombing case was presented. In this case, an FBI examiner reported that he was able to match a fingerprint from Brandon Mayfield to a partial print that was found at the scene of the bombing. His findings were subsequently confirmed by two additional FBI examiners and an independent examiner who was retained by Mayfield. All of the additional examiners confirmed the identification made by the first examiner. All of the additional examiners were in possession of the report and conclusions of the first and subsequent examiners. All four of the fingerprint examiners were wrong about their conclusions and this was most probably due, at least in part, to confirmational bias. Each examiner was predisposed to a match of the fingerprints because they knew that other examiners had found and confirmed this match. This is a classic case of confirmational bias.

Mechanisms for handling observer bias

There are a number of practices that can be put into place in a forensic science laboratory that can minimize or eliminate certain types of observer bias. Some of these can be expensive, cumbersome, and bureaucratic. The stakes, however, are high.

Virtually every field of scientific endeavor has measures built into its protocols to guard against bias in all of its practices so that the results and conclusions of experiments and studies can be relied upon as scientific. The forensic science community can demand and deliver no less, considering that life and liberty are at stake.

Lineups instead of showups

When an eyewitness to a crime is asked to identify the perpetrator, the suspect is shown to the witness behind a one-way mirror in the presence of other people who are similar in appearance. A half-dozen or so people including the suspect are put in a line and the witness is asked to pick out the correct person. This is a lineup and is familiar to everyone who watches police shows or movies. In most forensic cases, examiners are presented with showups; only one known that is to be compared with the unknown. The showup focuses attention on only one suspect or victim. A lineup of several similar known exhibits would take this bias out of the equation and force the examiner to base their conclusions on only the scientific data developed in the examination. Thus, in a fingerprint case, where a single print has been lifted from the crime scene, the examiner could be given not only the suspect's known prints but also those of other people whose prints are similar. The focus would be taken off the suspect's prints and put on the minutiae of the known and unknown sets of prints and make the comparison more objective. The same procedure could be followed with firearms, questioned document, shoeprint and tire tread markings, and other types of pattern evidence.

Blind testing and confirmation

It has been established that domain-irrelevant information can easily bias an examiner. Giving the examiner only the information needed to properly analyze the evidence is the best practice. Implementing this, however, can be difficult. First, what constitutes domain-irrelevant information must be defined for each case and for each area of forensic science. If ancillary information is to be withheld from individual examiners, there must be a way to link all of the examinations up at the end with all of the information available so that the complete story of the evidence can be told. One way of accomplishing this is to have a master case agent receive the evidence, determine what information each examiner needs, and then dole out the evidence to the examiners with only the relevant information. After the examiners finish their analyses, the master case agent collects the reports, and then links them up with all of the information. This protects each individual examiner from contamination and bias and still gives the evidence its due. If the lab has a practice of confirming conclusions by having another examiner reexamine the evidence, then the second scientist must not be given any information about the conclusions reached by the first one. Although all types of forensic science, including DNA typing, are subject to observer bias, the pattern evidence types discussed in this chapter are the most susceptible to these problems because their analyses depend almost completely upon the examiner's personal observations and opinions without any instrumental backup. This makes it critical for forensic scientists to recognize the evils of observer bias and put protocols into place that can eliminate or at least minimize it.

Conclusion

What have we learned about forensic science?

First, it is the quintessential multidisciplinary science. Nearly every scientific endeavor, including the social sciences, has some applications to the legal system of almost every country in the world. Most countries have forensic laboratories and crime scene investigators who collect and analyze scientific evidence and offer testimony in court. These systems differ in size, placement, and organization, depending upon the type of government and the level of crime.

Second, forensic science laboratories are, by and large, reactive. They generally do not take charge of the crime scene investigation; if laboratory personnel are involved, it is in a supporting role. In some countries, forensic scientists are routinely called out to certain crime scenes, especially clandestine drug laboratories and perhaps high-profile homicide cases.

Third, in many countries forensic science laboratories are part of the justice system, often part of a police department, which can create bias and affect how their science is viewed by the parent organization and the public.

Fourth, in many places, forensic science laboratories and scientists are insufficiently regulated. There is often no mandatory accreditation of crime laboratories, in stark contrast to medical and other scientific organizations. Likewise, forensic scientists are often not subject to any mandatory, systematic certification, again in contrast to medical and other scientific personnel. This has implications for the competence and accountability of scientists and laboratories.

This does not mean that no one is paying attention or that forensic science is not changing. Indeed, a number of trends encourage those who seek to make the system both more responsive to the needs of the public and more competent. There are several reasons for these recent and sometimes profound changes.

First, there have been an increasing number of highly publicized cases throughout the world, some of which have been mentioned in this book, in which forensic science and scientists have contributed to what can only be described as miscarriages of justice. Examples have come from the US, UK, Australia, Canada, and European countries; although they represent only a tiny minority of crimes, many of the cases have a high profile.

Another relatively recent phenomenon has been the use of DNA typing. First developed in the 1980s by Professor Alec Jeffreys of Leicester University, DNA typing has raised the standards for analysis of all forensic science evidence, revolutionized the ability to associate biological evidence with a person or object, allowed the reexamination of hundreds of convictions, and permitted the reopening of many cold cases. These cases have had a major impact on the media and the public.

The media, especially television, have also had major effects on forensic science and the judicial system, especially, but not only, in the United States. The *CSI* programs are watched throughout the world, raising the public's level of awareness of science and forensic science, and greatly increasing expectations about criminal investigation and forensic science. This has led to a huge expansion of university-level forensic science education, especially in the UK, where more than three hundred tertiary-level programs have "forensic" in their title.

High-profile cases and the development of DNA typing have caused scientists to reexamine traditional types of evidence, such as fingerprints, firearms, and handwriting, which have been accepted in courts all over the world for more than a hundred years. Recent court decisions have caused people to question the scientific validity of conclusions made by forensic examiners every day. There is little reliable empirical research into the validity and reliability of such evidence; some judges now question its admissibility for identification purposes, but the future will almost certainly bring new research.

In addition to the familiar areas of forensic science that have been discussed in this book, some new and emerging areas need to be carefully scrutinized. Among these are the behavioral forensic sciences, which include forensic psychology and psychiatry, psychological profiling, some types of crime scene reconstruction, and interrogation techniques such as polygraphy. Questions have arisen in the US and elsewhere about the validity of some of the conclusions reached by practitioners in these fields and how these "soft sciences" should be treated with respect to admissibility of evidence.

Probably the fastest-growing emerging area of forensic science is digital forensics: a catchall title for a number of areas of study including computer forensics (the use of computers both for committing and solving crimes), imaging, and biometrics. Computer crime is one of the most common types of crime; digital forensic scientists are working overtime to keep up with cyber-criminals. The field of biometrics, in which various physical features are documented, is supplementing traditional identification methods, such as fingerprinting, to associate people with crimes in a more scientific, defendable way. The imaging of everything from fingerprints to faces has become critically important as a law enforcement tool.

There is little question that forensic science will continue its explosive growth and become increasingly important as a suite of tools that can effectively help to fight crime worldwide. As crime becomes more global, so must the search for, and use of, scientific evidence. Science can be a powerful tool but its use must be coordinated and continually advanced to keep up with modern criminals and their crimes.

Further reading

Jackson, R.W. and Jackson, J.M., *Forensic Science*, Prentice Hall, Englewood Cliffs, NJ, 2004

James, S.H. and Nordby, J.J. (eds), *Forensic Science: An Introduction to Scientific and Investigative Techniques*, 3rd edition, Taylor & Francis Group, Boca Raton, FL, 2012

Saferstein, R., *Criminalistics: An Introduction to Forensic Science*, Prentice Hall, Englewood Cliffs, NJ, 2014

Siegel, J. and Houck, M., *Fundamentals of Forensic Science*, 2nd edition, Elsevier, Burlington, MA, 2010

Siegel, J. and Mirakovits, K., *Forensic Science: The Basics*, 2nd edition, Taylor & Francis Group, Boca Raton, FL, 2010

Siegel, J. and Sauko, P. (eds.), *Encyclopedia of Forensic Science*, 2nd edition, vols. 1–4, Academic Press, St. Louis, MO, 2012

Thorwald, J., *Century of the Detective*, Harcourt Brace & World, New York, 1964

Index

References to images are in *italics*.

abused drugs 45, 46–57
accelerants 72–3, 74, 82
agglutination 148
alcohol 60–1, 119–20, 121
algor mortis 121, 122
alleles 156, 158, 163
alpha-amylase test 150
American Academy of Forensic
    Sciences (AAFS) 7, 8
analysis 2–4, 5–6, 24–5, 209–10
    and blood 145–7
    and body fluids 149–51
    and DNA 157–63, *164*
    and drugs 55–7, 62–3
    and explosions 80–2
    and fibers 88–9
    and fire 74
    and glass 102, 104–7
    and hair 201–4
    and paint 96–8
anatomic pathology 114
ANFO 66, 76, 80
animals 133, 134, 146–7, 200
annealing 161
anthropology 3–4, 112–13, 114, 124,
    131–8
anthropometry 175
antibodies 146–7, 148
antigens 146, 147–8
antiserum 147
appeals 29
arson 66–7, 68–9, 70–4, 82
arthropods 124, 125–6, 128–31
artistic paints 93, 94
Ashworth, Dawn 142

asphyxiation 120
Atlanta Child Murderer 84
Australia 11–12, 13
Automated Fingerprint Identification
    Systems (AFIS) 183–5
automative paints 93, 95–7, 98
autopsies 116–17

ballistics 185–6
barbiturates 50, 60–1
Bendectin 36–7
Bertillon, Alphonse 175
bias 212–18
binders 91, 92, 94, 97, 98
biological profiles 133, 134–7
biometrics 221
bite marks 139, 141
black powder 76, 189
blood 18, 20, 85, 142, 143, 144–8
    and DNA 160
blood spatter 143–4, 166–9
blowflies 124, 126–7
blunt force injuries 118
body fluids 117, 143, 148–9; *see also*
    blood; semen
bombs 66, 76, 78, *79*, 80–2, 170–1
bones 3–4, 132–8
borosilicate glass 101
botany 113
Bowman, Margaret 139
buccal samples 160
Buckland, Richard 142, 143
bullets 24, 25, 118, 185, 188–9,
    190–2
Bundy, Theodore 139

Bureau of Alcohol, Tobacco, Firearms and Explosives (BATF) 10
burglaries 21, 31, 93, 174

cannabis, *see* marijuana
capillary electrophoresis 162–3, *164*
carbon monoxide 120
cars 93, 95–6
cartridge cases 185, 189–90, 190, 192
chain of custody 26, 151
Chartered Society of Forensic Sciences (FSS) 7, 8–9
chemical injury 118, 119–20
chips 95–6, 97
Christmas tree stain 149
chromosomes 155
Circuit Courts 29
circumstantial evidence 6, 84
civil courts 124
class evidence 24–5, 26, 86, 98, 201, 203
clinical pathology 115
clothing 99, 117, 121, 122, 128
   and protective 159
coatings 91, 92
cocaine 3, 48–9, 120, 131, 197–8
   and tests 56, 57
cold searches 16
color 107, 110
Combined DNA Index System (CODIS) 165
combustion 67–8, 69, 75, 82, 189
comparison microscopes 191, 202
competence 31
computers 183–4, 193, 221
confirmational bias 5, 171, 216
contamination 17, 18–19, 26, 159
controlled substances 45, 46–57
Coors, Adolph 108–9
coroners 16, 115, 116
cortex 199–200, 202
Court of Appeal 29
courtrooms 27, 28–39, 42–4, 208–8
crack 49
credentials 207–8
crime scene investigation (CSI) 2–3, 4–6, 26, 219
   and anthropology 138

and entomology 125–6
and fingerprints 179, 182
and hair 201
and process 16, 17–19
criminal investigation 5, 15–17
criminal sexual conduct (CSC) 149, 150–1, 160
Crown Court 28–9
CSI (TV show) 6–7, 220
cuticles 199, 201–2
cyber-crime 221

dactyloscopy 174, 177–8; *see also* fingerprints
Daoud, Ouhnane 171
Darwin, Charles 174–5
Daubert v. Merrell Dow case 36–9, 173
decomposition 123–4, 127–9
defense attorneys 7, 29, 30, 207
deflagrations 75–6, 82
demonstrative evidence 20
density 106–7
depressants 50
detonations 76–82
digital forensics 221
District Courts 28
DNA 1, 23, 26, 113, 142–3, 151–2, 154–5
   and analysis 157–63, *164*
   and cellular 155–7
   and databases 164–5
   and definition 152–4
   and hair 204
   and mitochondria 166–7
   and reexamination 220
Dobson, Gary 85
documentation 18, 26, 28
dogs 73
domain-irrelevant information 215, 217–18
double helix 153, *154*
Drug Enforcement Administration (DEA) 9–10, 55
drugs 20, 24–5, 45–55, 210
   and administration 58–62
   and analysis 55–7
   and arthropods 130–1
   and death 119–20

and hair 197–8
and workplace testing 62–4
dry-labbing 12, 210
dynamite 77

electrical injury 118, 120
elimination samples 159
entomology 113, 124–31
epidemiology 36–7
error rates 38
ethics 13, 206–12
and bias 212–18
evidence 2–3, 5–7, 15, 19–27
and admissibility 32–4, 37–8
and DNA 157–9, 165
and documentation 18–19
and entomology 129–31
and hair 201
and malpractice 12–13
and rules 29–31, 34–6, 43–4
and sexual crime 150–1
and soil 109–10
see also class evidence; pattern
evidence; trace evidence
excavation 17, 18, 19, 138
exemplars 193–5
exotherimic reactions 67
expert witnesses 4, 27, 28, 42–4,
207–8
and evidence 32, 33
explosions 66, 67–8, 74–82

facial features 132
facial reconstruction 137–8
falsifiability 38
Faulds, Henry 174–5
Federal Bureau of Investigation
(FBI) 9, 84, 108–9, 163, 165
and fingerprints 170–1, 177, 184,
216
Federal Rules of Evidence (FREs)
34–6, 37–8
fibers 20, 21–2, 84, 85–91, 98
fingerprints 20, 21, 23, 173–4, 177–9
and automated identification 183–5
and comparison 181–3
and FBI 170–1, 216
and history 174–7

and visualization 179–81
fire 66–71, 74–5, 82
and investigation 71–4
fire triangle 69–70
firearms 23, 25, 118–19, 185–92
Fletcher, Yvonne 18
float glass 101
fluorescein 146
Forensic Science Committee 173
forgery 93, 196–7
Forsyth, Alexander John 189
fracture matches 102, *103*, 104
Frye case 33, 34, 36, 37, 38–9
fuel 67–8, 69–70, 72, 75, 77, 82

Galton, Sir Francis 175–6
gasoline 68, 72
gender 135–6
general acceptance standard 34, 38–9
genes 155–6, 166
glass 21–2, 98, 99, 100–7
Glass Refractive Index Measurement
(GRIM) 106
Griess test 81
grooves 187–9
gunpowder 185
gunshot wounds 118–19, 130

hair 84, 85, 86, 130, 197–8
and analysis 63–4, 201–4
and DNA 204
and genes 155–6
and structure 198–200
half-lives 59–60
hallucinogens 50–3
handwriting 23, 192–7
Hastie fire 66–7
Haversian canals 134
hemoglobin 146
Henry, Sir Edward 176–7
Henry system 182
heroin 54–5
Herschel, William 174
high explosives 76–7, 78, 82
hit-and-run accidents 21–2, 99
Homeland Security Department 10
hot searches 16
House of Lords 29

human body parts 112–14
humus 107
hyperthermia 120–1
hypothermia 121

identification 112–14, 116, 175
 and fingerprints 182–5
 and odontology 139–40, 141
 and skeletal remains 132, 133–8
illicit drugs 3, 45–6, 46–57
immunoprecipitation 146–7
Improvised Explosive Devices
 (IEDs) 78
incendiary fires 70–1, 73–4
individualization 23–6
inductively coupled plasma mass
 spectrometer (ICP/MS) 104
injuries 117–21
inquests 115
insects 113, 121, 124, 125–7, 129–30
instars 127
Integrated Automated Fingerprint
 Identification System
 (IAFIS) 170–1, 184
Internal Revenue Service (IRS) 10
International Association for
 Identification 182–3
International Association of Forensic
 Sciences 8
iodine fuming 179–80

Jeffreys, Dr. Alex 142–3, 220
judges 30, 207
jurors 4, 6, 7, 29, 30, 33
 and expert witnesses 43
Justice Department 9–10
justice system 206–7, 219

Kappen, Joseph 165
known evidence 20–2, 26

laboratories 9–14, 209–10, 219
 and reports 39–41, 44, 210–12
lands 187–9
lasers 181
latent prints 170–1, 177, 179
Lawrence, Stephen 85
Lee, Bruce 67

Levine, Dr. Lowell 139
Levy, Lisa 139
Libyan Embassy 18
licit drugs 45–6
lineups 217
livor mortis 121, 122–3
locus 155, 158, 163
low explosives 76, 78, 80, 82
LSD 52–3, 59, 62
luminol 146
lysing 160

machine guns 186
maggots 112, *126*, 127, 129, 130–1
Magistrate's Court 28, 29
Mann, Lynda 142
marijuana 18–19, 50–2, 61–2, 120
 and tests 56–7, 210
mass disasters 132, 139, 141
mass spectrometry 56, 63, 104, 130
material evidence 31
Mayfield, Brandon 170, 171, 216
Meadow, Sir Roy 13
mechanical injury 118
medical examiners 16
medullae 200, 202
melanin 198
mercury fulminate 189–90
Merritt, Dr. Richard 130–1
metabolites 60
methamphetamine 45, 49–50, 61
microcrystals 146
microtomes 97
Misuse of Drugs Act (1971) 46
mitochondrial DNA 166–7
Molotov Cocktails 102, *103*, 104
Morin case 13
morphine 53–4
morphology 87, 88

narcotics 3, 53–5
National Automated Fingerprint
 Identification System
 (NAFIS) 182
National Crime Information Center
 (NCIC) 184
National DNA Database
 (NDNAD) 164–5

National Institute for Standards and
    Technology (NIST) 184
natural fibers 88
negative controls 159
negative pressure phase 78, *79*, 80
ninhydrin 180
nitrates 81
nitroglycerine 77, 82
non-requested writing 194–5
Norris, David 85

observer bias 171, 213–18, 216–17
odontology 1, 113, 131, 139–41;
    see also teeth
Oklahoma City bombing 66, 76
opium 53–4
Osborne, Walter 108–9
osteology 131
oxygen 67–8, 69–70, 75, 77, 81, 82

paint 21–2, 91–8
patent prints 177, 179
pathology 113, 114–15, 131, 116–21
    and post-mortems 121–4
pattern evidence 167–9, 172–3, 204–5,
    213
PCR (polymerase chain reaction) 160–2
peels 97
peer reviews 34, 38, 208
pelvis 135–6
perforating wounds 118
PETN 77
pharmacology 58, 59
photographic superimposition 137
photography 18, 20, 117, 139
pigments 91, 92, 94, 95, 98
pistols 186
Pitchfork, Colin 143
plastic explosives 77
plastic prints 177, 179
plexiform bone 134
points of origin 71, 72, 73–4, 82
    and explosions 78, 80–1
police 3, 5, 15–17, 212–13, 219
polygraphs 20, 33, 221
polymerase extension 161
polymorphic materials 147, 148,
    151–2, 154–5, 156–7

population frequency 158
portrait parlé 175
positive controls 159
positive pressure phase 78, *79*, 80
post-mortem interval (PMI) 16, 112,
    113–14, 121–4, 125, 126
probability 157–8
product rule 158
professional development 208–9
prosecutors 6, 13, 17, 29, 30
prostate-specific antigen (PSA) 150
psychology 221
putrefaction 123

Queen's Court 29
questioned documents 192–7

race 136
Rajesh, Gupta 99
rape kits 151
refractive index 104–6
regulation 219
requested writing 193–4
Rhodamine 6G 181
ridgeology 174
rifles 186
rigor mortis 121, 122
Rogerson, Mary Jane 112
Ruxton, Isabella 112–13

saliva 143, 150
sand 99, 100
scale drawings 18, 20
screening tests 55–7, 63
search patterns 17–18
Secret Service (USSS) 10
semen 142, 143, 149–50
seminal acid phosphatase (SAP)
    149–50
Sensabaugh, George 149–50
serology 113, 142, 143, 144–8
sharp force injuries 118
shoeprints 15, 98, 100, 108
short tandem repeats (STR) 161,
    162–3
shotguns 187
showups 214–15, 217
shrapnel 78

signatures 192–3, 194, 196
silver nitrate 180
Simpson, O.J. 2
situational bias 212–13
skeletal remains 131–8
skulls 132, 136, 137
smears 95, 96
smokeless powder 189
soil 98, 107–11
Souviron, Dr. Richard 139
sperm 149, 160
Splatt case 13
statistics 37
stimulants 48–50
"sting" operations 16
stippling 119
stomach contents 123
stria 188–9, 191–2
structural paints 93
submachine guns 186
subpoenas 28
substrate control 160
Super Glue® fuming 179, 180–1
Superior Courts 29
Supreme Court 29, 37–8
suspects 17, 21, 214–15, 217
    and DNA 165
    and fingerprints 181–2
suspensions 91–2
synergism 60–1, 119–20
synthetic fibers 88
synthetic marijuana 52
Systolic Blood Pressure Deception
    Test 33, 34

Takayama test 146
tear matches 88–9
teeth 1, 135, 139, 140–1
Teichmann test 146
temperature 121–2, 128
tempered glass 101
terminology 211–12
terrorism 76, 78, 80–1, 141, 170–1
testimonial evidence 20
textile fibers 86–7, 88
thermal injury 118, 120–1
thermocycler 161–2

tinted glass 101–2, 107
tires 98, 100, 108, 109
TNT 77
toolmarks 23, 185–6
toxic tort 36
toxicology 58–62, 115, 117, 130
trace evidence 85–6, 98, 102, 110–11,
    190
tracing 196–7
transfer 90–1
trials 29–39, 42–4
triers of fact 4, 30

Uniform Controlled Substances Act
    (1969) 47
United Kingdom 7, 8–9, 28–9, 46–7,
    164–5
United States of America 7, 9–11,
    28–9, 34–6, 116, 165
    and admissibility 33–4, 37–8
    and drugs 47, 49, 52, 54, 55
unknown evidence 20–2, 26
urea nitrate 80–1
urine testing 62–4
US Fish and Wildlife Service
    (USFWS) 10–11
US Postal Service (USPS) 11

vaginal secretions 150
victims 15–16
violent deaths 117–21
visualization 179–81
voir dire 42, 43
Vucetich, Juan 176

West, William 175
Williams, Wayne 84
witnesses 16, 20, 29, 30, 43
    and suspects 214–15, 217
    see also expert witnesses
workplace drug testing 62–4
World Trade Center 80, 132, 141
wounds 117, 118–19, 130

X-rays 114, 117, 137, 141

Zain, Fred 12